ONE JESUIT'S

SPIRITUAL JOURNEY

OTHER BOOKS BY PEDRO ARRUPE, S.J.
available from
The Institute of Jesuit Sources

Challenge to Religious Life Today.
Selected Letters and Addresses—I.   1979, 310 pages.

Justice with Faith Today.
Selected Letters and Addresses—II.   1980, 336 pages.

Other Apostolates Today.
Selected Letters and Addresses—III.   1981, 382 pages.

*In Him Alone Is Our Hope. Texts on the Heart of Christ
(1965-1983).* Foreword by Karl Rahner, S.J.

Selected Letters and Addresses—IV.   1984, 180 pages.

PEDRO ARRUPE, S.J.

ONE JESUIT'S SPIRITUAL JOURNEY

*Autobiographical Conversations
with Jean-Claude Dietsch, S.J.*

Selected Letters and Addresses—V

Translated by Ruth Bradley

THE INSTITUTE OF JESUIT SOURCES
St. Louis, 1986

in cooperation with
Gujarat Sahitya Prakash
Anand, India.

This book is an authorized translation of Pedro Arrupe, *Itinéraire d'un Jésuite. Entretiens avec Jean-Claude Dietsch, S.J.*, published and copyrighted in 1982 by Editions du Centurion, 17 rue de Babylone, 75007 Paris, France.

JRC
BX
3703
.A77
1986
v.5
c.4

This is the
First Edition, for the Americas, Europe, and Australia.

Note: There is a *Second Edition,* authorized for
sale only in Asia and Africa, which
can be ordered from Gujarat Sahitya Prakash,
Anand 388 001, India.

All rights reserved
Printed in the United States of America
Library of Congress Catalog Card Number: 84-81990
ISBN 0-912422-69-6   Cloth
ISBN 0-912422-68-8   Smyth sewn paperback

CONTENTS

EDITOR'S FOREWORD

Father Pedro Arrupe lived in many continents and witnessed many crucial events of contemporary world history. He was in Europe at the time of the expulsion of the Jesuits from Spain in 1932, the civil war in Spain, and the rise of Nazism in Germany; in Japan during World War II and in Hiroshima when the atomic bomb exploded there; and back in Europe where he lived in Rome during the last session of Vatican Council II, and after that for the period of renewal but also of controversies within the post-Conciliar Church. As Superior General of the Jesuits from May 22, 1965, until he was disabled by a stroke on August 7, 1981, he was intimately associated with many officials of the Church's curia in Rome, with Bishops from all the world, with Superiors General of many religious institutes of women and men, and with other important persons of ecclesiastical and civil life. Thus he had a role of no small importance in shaping the thought currents and other developments of the post-Conciliar era.

Between Christmas of 1980 and Easter of 1981 he granted to Father Jean-Claude Dietsch, then Director of the Press and Information Office in the Jesuit Curia, a series of autobiographical interviews. They were published in France in 1982 and are now published here in English by the Institute of Jesuit Sources for America, Europe, and Australia, and by Gujarat Sahitya Prakash (Gujarat language for "Gujarat Source of Light") for the rest of the world.

As he recounts details of his "zigzagged journey" before his election as General and of his life in Rome after it, his simultaneous spiritual journey with the Lord more and more emerges from the pages. He narrates his story in a conversational manner with the openness, spontaneity, and simplicity which are characteristic of him. His book reveals the functioning of his mind as well as the inspirational and spiritual ideas which impelled him as he guided and governed the Society of Jesus in those transitional post-Conciliar years. The book is therefore interesting because it discloses the interior wellsprings of a fascinating personality. But beyond that, in future years it will also be important for historians and others who will have need to recount and interpret the events in his generalate.

Dr. Ruth Bradley, who teaches French in the Department of Foreign Languages of the University of Southwestern Louisiana, Lafayette, Louisiana, kindly volunteered to translate the book. As editor, the present writer asked her how she became interested in it. The letter she wrote in reply was so interesting and brought out so many new facets of my remarks made above about Father Arrupe that it has seemed wise to me to pass most of it along to our readers.

"The book first fell into my hands in the summer of 1982 when I was working in Angers, France, at the Université Catholique de l'Quest. I went to a local bookstore to buy a gift for a student of mine, a young Jesuit novice who was about to pronounce his Jesuit vows in August. There I found a copy of the *Itinéraire* and purchased it. I began reading it in my room that evening and next day I returned to the bookstore and bought another copy for myself.

"I was profoundly moved, as I read it, by the humility and simplicity of Pedro Arrupe, who was, indeed, one of the very important men in today's Church. I think the only other thing I had read about him was the *Time* feature article entitled 'The Black Pope.'

"Just two years before, I had made the complete Spiritual Exercises of St. Ignatius for thirty days under the direction of Father A. Patrick Phillips at the Jesuit Spirituality Center in Grand Coteau, Louisiana. The thing that made the deepest impression on me as I read Father Arrupe's book was the fact that this man's entire life reflected a living out of St. Ignatius' *Spiritual Exercises* in every detail. *Intinéraire* was a book that had something to say to me

viii

as I tried to shape my life as a laywoman to the ideals of Ignatius. I often think I don't do very well at this as I live out my life in our marketplace world. But Father Arrupe too was living out his life in dealing with prominent persons of Church, state, and marketplace; and somehow that has its similarities to the business world, the academic world, the world of work in which we all find ourselves in this final quarter of the twentieth century.

"In other words, I felt I was meeting a man who was a saint for our times and I stated that during a dinner at the Jesuit Spirituality Center shortly after I returned from France to Louisiana. I also mentioned that I thought the work ought to be translated into English. Father Phillips asked me why I did not do it myself. Brother George A. Murphy, who was at the table with us, wrote to a friend of his and learned that the contract for it was under consideration by a publisher in England. I thought no more about the matter. But several months later Brother Murphy called, saying that things had not worked out with the British publisher; and then he put me in contact with you in St. Louis.

"You know the rest. As I have told you, this was indeed a labor of love. As I translated I was trying to capture the spirit and personality of the man who was coming through to me, so that the English-speaking reader could perceive Father Arrupe's spirit and meet him personally as a warm and deeply spiritual man. I hope and pray that the seeds sown by the English work will bear much fruit. Of course, I realize too that the book is a valuable source of information for historians both of the universal Church and of the Society."

The Institute of Jesuit Sources expresses its gratitude to Doctor Bradley for completing this work and telling us the spirit in which she did it.

George E. Ganss, S.J.
Director and General Editor
The Institute of Jesuit Sources
January 1, 1985

A NOTE OF THANKS FROM THE TRANSLATOR

The translator wishes to express special gratitude to Father Patrick Phillips, S.J., Director of the Jesuit Spirituality Center in Grand Coteau, Louisiana, without whose spiritual guidance this work would never have been undertaken, and to Father George Ganss, S.J., for his encouragement and shared enthusiasm for the project. Thanks are also due to Brother George Murphy, S.J., whose interest in the work brought the translator into contact with the Institute of Jesuit Sources, to many friends for their prayers and support, and to Mrs. Julie Cavalier and Mrs. Claudette Landry who typed the final manuscript of the English text.

The translator is also grateful to Le Centurion, the publisher in Paris of the French book in 1982, for a list of small corrections to be made on pages 12, 118, 128, 129, 131, and 134 of that French text. Those alterations have been followed in the English version.

Ruth Bradley
University of Southwestern Louisiana
Lafayette, Louisiana
November 1, 1984

A PRELIMINARY NOTE

The interviews which constitute the main part of this book, along with some quotations from texts and conferences, took place between Christmas 1980 and Easter 1981.

Since then, many events have marked the life of the Church and of the Society of Jesus: the attempted assassination of His Holiness John Paul II Wednesday, May 13, 1981; the cerebral thrombosis which struck Father Arrupe on August 7, 1981; the nomination, in October 1981, of Father Dezza as Delegate of the Holy Father at the head of the Society to prepare it for a future General Congregation and, in view of Father Arrupe's state of health, to see to the everyday government of the Order.

These interviews represent, therefore, a particular moment in the life of Father Arrupe and in the history of the Society of Jesus; they could not, evidently, take into consideration the most recent developments in either the one or the other, since after his stroke Father Arrupe could not resume the work of interviewing and editing.

Furthermore, in revising one last time these pages early in 1982, we have kept the present tense where a historian would expect perhaps a past tense, since Father Arrupe today in 1982 no longer exercises the responsibilities which were his at the time of the interviews. But we desire this book to be a kind of echo of Father Arrupe's own speech, warmth, energy, and spontaneity. Until a successor of his will be elected, he still remains the Superior General of the Society of Jesus;[1] and one does not change the grammatical tense of an echo.

Jean-Claude Dietsch, S.J.

1 [The French original of this book was published in 1982, while Father Arrupe was still general, although greatly impeded by his ill health. He officially resigned his office on September 3, 1983, and his successor, Father Peter-Hans Kolvenbach, was elected superior general on September 13, 1983. Editor.]

A BIOGRAPHICAL SKETCH

Pedro Arrupe was born in Bilbao, Spain, on November 14, 1907. His father was a founder of one of the first Catholic newspapers in Spain, *La Gaceta del Norte.*

He gave up his medical studies at the University of Madrid to enter the Society of Jesus on January 15, 1927. When the Spanish government ordered the expulsion of the Order's 2,640 members from its realms in February, 1932, he left Spain and continued his studies in Belgium, Holland, and the United States. He was ordained a priest on July 30, 1936.

In 1938 he went to Japan as a missionary. He was later named Master of Novices and then Rector of the novitiate. At the time of the explosion of the first atomic bomb on August 6, 1945, he was in Hiroshima. Along with his novices, he devoted himself without counting the cost to the care of the wounded, turning the novitiate into a makeshift hospital. In 1954 he was named director of the vice-province of Japan; and when, on October 18, 1959, Japan was made a province, he was named its provincial, a position he filled until 1965. Under his direction, the Catholic University of Tokyo was greatly expanded; it had 1,500 students in 1945 and now counts 6,000. He published several books on Ignatian spirituality in Japanese, and related his memories of Hiroshima in a book published in Spanish.

On May 22, 1965, the 218 Jesuit Fathers representing the 36,000 members of the order in 90 countries who were gathered in Rome for their 31st General Congregation elected Father Arrupe, on the third ballot, the Superior General of the Society of Jesus.

Father Arrupe has traveled extensively in Europe, Africa, Asia, and North and South America. He speaks Spanish, Italian, English, French, German, Japanese, and Latin.

It was on his return from a trip to the Philippines on August 7, 1981, that he was striken with a cerebral thrombosis. In spite of a definite improvement in his health, it was still impossible for him to reread and complete the text of these conversational interviews.[1]

1 [Numerous collections of letters, addresses, and the like by Father Pedro Arrupe have been published in various languages. Four volumes of them are presently available in English in the series of "Selected Letters and Addresses." They are copublished by the Institute of Jesuit Sources, St. Louis, Missouri, U.S.A. for North America, and by Gujarat Sahitya Prakash (Gujarat language for "Gujarat Source of Light), Anand Press, Gujarat 388001, India for the rest of the world:

> *Challenge to Religious Life Today.* Selected Letters and Addresses—I.
> 1979, 310 pages.
>
> *Justice with Faith Today.* Selected Letters and Addresses—II.
> 1980, 336 pages.
>
> *Other Apostolates Today.* Selected Letters and Addresses—III.
> 1981, 382 pages.
>
> *In Him Alone Is Our Hope: Texts on the Heart of Christ* (1965-1983).
> Foreword by Karl Rahner, S.J. Selected Letters and Addresses—IV.
> 1984, 180 pages.

Some of the titles are slightly different in India. The series name is "An Anthology of Letters and Addresses." No. III is *Jesuit Apostolates Today.* No. IV is *Legacy of the Heart: Texts on the Heart of Christ.*

The present volume, *One Jesuit's Spiritual Journey,* is published by the Institute of Jesuit Sources for the Americas, Europe, Australia, and New Zealand, and by Gujarat Sahitya Prakash for Asia and Africa. Editor.]

ONE JESUIT'S
SPIRITUAL JOURNEY

ABBREVIATIONS

used in the footnotes

ActRSJ   *Acta Romana Societatis Iesu*

Cons   St. Ignatius' *Constitutions of the Society of Jesus*

EppIgn   *S. Ignatii Epistolae et Instructiones,* 12 volumes in MHSJ

FN   *Fontes Narrativi de S. Ignatio de Loyola,* 4 volumes in MHSJ

LettersIgn *Letters of St. Ignatius,* translated by W.J. Young, S.J.

MHSJ   The series Monumenta Historica Societatis Iesu, 124 volumes

MonNad   *Epistolae et Monumenta P. Hieronymi Nadal,* 6 volumes in MHSJ

SpEx   The *Spiritual Exercises of St. Ignatius of Loyola*

Chapter 1

THE INTERVIEWER'S INTRODUCTION

It may come as a surprise to the reader that it was a Jesuit who conducted this series of interviews with Very Reverend Father Pedro Arrupe, and who asked his Superior General to tell him the story of his life; to tell him and to explain what were, at different periods of life, and what are today his points of reference, his criteria, his major points of orientation; to express how he reacted to the recent changes in the world and in the Church and how he assesses their situation today; to indicate which paths he himself followed in order to lead, according to the spirit of St. Ignatius, the thousands of Jesuits who, throughout the world, carry out such diverse apostolic tasks.

Would it not have been preferable to choose a non-Jesuit interviewer, whose different background would justify the curiosity, the insistence, the astonishment and lack of understanding, the persistence for "finding out more"?—in short, an interviewer who would feel more free to interrupt the discourse, to probe the words and the ideas in order to put their profound strength to the proof, to contest this or that interpretation, and to bring up opposing views, including those of a nonbeliever?

As a Jesuit, have I asked the type of questions that will allow the readers to discover who Father Arrupe is and to hear his testimony as a man, as a Christian, as a priest, as a religious? These questions, would they appear falsely naive, complacent, even leading? Would I be suspect of having avoided certain subjects, or having sidetracked the difficulties while giving the impression of facing them?

As I listen, once more, to the twelve cassettes on which the answers of Father Arrupe were taped between Christmas 1980 and

Easter 1981, I am very confident that such scruples are unnecessary. The interviews represent neither an evaluation nor an appeal nor an apologetic discourse. They are strictly the expression of a life rich in experiences, of a manner of thinking nurtured by prayer and meditation, and of a life story inspired by attentive listening to the Divine Will. The guide in this "spiritual journey" is certainly not the interviewer asking the questions. Dare I say that the one who answers them is not the guide either? Some One else appears, Who was and remains, in every moment of the life of Father Arrupe, Someone sought, met, heard, and followed. During our interviews, whatever my questions might have been, it was to Him that the conversation came back, since to my interlocutor "Jesus Christ is everything."

Stated as a fact which should need no explanation, this brief formula summarizes, in effect, all the experience of the person who speaks it, like the confessions of faith of the first Christian communities. Often, as a matter of fact, while listening to Father Arrupe, I thought of the Acts of the Apostles, an unchanging picture of a living Church, close to its Lord Christ and open to the rich diversity of the people.

The theological and spiritual explanation will come later. A formula like this is, first of all, a cry of recognition towards the Christ one has met and loved, a sign of recognition among those who share the same faith, and also a recognition of the apostolic view that all men are called to be saved. One same word, recognition, for three complementary views: It is clear that, for Father Arrupe, his personal history, his life in the heart of the Church and of the Society of Jesus, and his work in the midst of the men of our time are nurtured, in prayer, loyalty, and obedience, by **thanksgiving**. He likes to recite these words from Sirach (51:1-2):

> I will give thanks to you, Lord and King,
> and praise you, God my savior,
> I give thanks to your name;
> for you have been protector and support to me.

Also, during the Eucharistic concelebration which marked the fiftieth anniversary of his entrance into the Society, he expressed himself thus:

"[I feel] amazement and gratitude not only for those privileged, decisive, and remarkable moments in my life, but also and above all for the innumerable graces which God never stopped bestowing on me during the past, all through a life otherwise very monotonous and ordinary. That is what causes me to wish that my life were or, at least, will be from now on a perpetual Magnificat."

"These privileged, decisive, and remarkable moments in my life" and "a life otherwise very monotonous and ordinary"—these two expressions call for comments on my part as the listener during the many hours which Father Arrupe devoted to this interview. Furthermore, consideration must be taken of the fact that I have been working by his side for more than three years. These expressions illustrate, at least partially, the atmosphere in which our talks took place and their evolution from one week to the next, as well as the manner in which I transcribed the sequence of questions and answers.

A brief biographical sketch is necessary at this point. Indeed, to impose a strictly chronological order upon this work would have impoverished an essential characteristic of our interviews. A word, a question, an image, or a memory would spontaneously suggest to Father Arrupe a bond between some of those "privileged, decisive, and remarkable moments" in his life, as well as between those moments and the profound convictions which sustain him spiritually and guide him. I felt it my duty to respect this spiritual method, this unifying vision of different manifestations of Divine Providence in a life which considers itself "otherwise very monotonous and ordinary." I have, therefore, respected as much as possible Father Arrupe's own dynamic thought and the succession of themes such as they occurred from one meeting to the next. That is why a reminder of certain dates and certain points of reference is useful in this Introduction.

Father Arrupe was born on November 14, 1907, in Bilbao, Spain. This origin does not justify the legend that Father Arrupe speaks the Basque language fluently. Though he understands Basque and likes to use some typical expressions, he also reminds us, not without humor, that, for that language more than for any other, he needs an interpreter. It can be pointed out at this time that, besides Spanish, he speaks English, French, German, Japanese, Italian, and Latin.

His father was an architect and participated in the founding of the daily newspaper *La Gaceta del Norte* because of his religious convictions. Here, again, it is an exaggeration to say that Father Arrupe has "journalism in his blood." His father was much more concerned with the financial aspects of the publication than with the professional qualifications of its writers (which, by the way, were excellent); and he did not hestitate, at the closing of the spiritual retreats which he used to attend regularly, to get his picture taken holding "his" newspaper well within the range of the camera.

Following his secondary schooling, Father Arrupe began his medical studies, first in Valladolid, then in Madrid. Some loyal friendships he has today date back to that time.

On January 15, 1927, he entered the novitiate of the Society of Jesus at Loyola, near the house where St. Ignatius was born. In 1932, after the Jesuit communities had been expelled from Spain, he continued his philosophical and theological studies, first in Marneffe, Belgium, and then in Valkenburg, Holland, where he was ordained as a priest in 1936. We find him a year later in the United States, where he completed his theological education at St. Mary's College, Kansas, and where he worked on a specialization in "medicine and psychiatry."

In June 1938 he left the United States for Japan—a departure which was the result, we discover in this book, of a persistent effort. After a period of preliminary apprenticeship, he was named parish priest of Yamaguchi. There, suspected of espionage for Western powers, he spent thirty-five days in prison, in solitary confinement.

In 1942 he became superior of the Yamaguchi district and Master of Novices and Rector of the Nagatsuka novitiate on the outskirts of Hiroshima. On August 6, 1945, he witnessed the explosion of the atomic bomb and organized immediately, with his novices, the first emergency assistance.

In March, 1954, he was called upon to govern the vice-province of the Society of Jesus in Japan, and, when it became a province in October, 1958, he was named the Provincial Superior.

On May 22, 1965, the members of the 31st General Congregation of the Society of Jesus elected Father Arrupe as Superior General. It is in that capacity that he participated in the Fourth Session of the Second Vatican Council.

In 1974-1975 he presided at the 32nd General Congregation, which he himself summoned, as well as the Congregations of the Procurators in 1970 and 1978.

In 1967, 1969, 1971, 1974, 1977 and 1980, he participated in the Synods of Bishops which took place in Rome.

Since 1967 he has been President of the Union of Major Superiors of Religious Orders, having been elected to the post in 1979 for the fifth consecutive time. He is also a member of the Sacred Congregation for the Evangelization of Peoples, a member of the General Council of the Pontifical Commission for Latin America, and Vice Grand Chancellor of the Pontifical Gregorian University, of the Pontifical Biblical Institute, and of the Pontifical Institute of Oriental Studies.

In the last few years, Father Arrupe has participated and spoken effectively at the International Eucharistic Congress of August 1976 in Philadelphia; at the November 1977 Inter-American Conference of Priests in Montreal; at the Conference of the Latin American Bishops, in Puebla in January of 1979; as well as at the General Assemblies of the Episcopal Conferences of Africa and Madagascar.

As Superior General, Father Arrupe has visited members of the Society of Jesus in almost every part of the world. Thus, in 1980, he met with superiors and communities in Nepal, India, Malaysia, in various African countries, in North America, in Cuba, as well as in France, Italy, Spain, and Germany.

It was upon his return from a fifteen-day trip to the Philippines, on the occasion of the 400th anniversary of the Jesuits' arrival in that country, that Father Arrupe was stricken by a cerebral thrombosis at the Fiumicino Airport of Rome. In spite of the definite improvement in his health, he was not able to reread these pages in their final form.

This biographical sketch, although very brief, indicates that in following Father Arrupe we will cover vast territories. We will meet, at least in thought, a multitude of men. We will relive a great variety of events and, above all, we will have a share in a very meaningful churchly experience which has been very diverse and wide-open to the difficulties and aspirations of our contemporaries—all this as we review a life whose only reason for being is Jesus Christ. But precisely because that life belongs to a "companion of Jesus," it cannot be expressed in the ordinary biographical manner. For Father Arrupe, what comes first is not himself in his individuality but his relationship to God; what he has received from Him and how he has used His gifts.

Only after acknowledging Divine Province, whose interventions he points out to us—he repeats like a litany of thanksgivings the names of cities that recall such interventions in his lifetime—and after exhaustively coming to the reason why, for him, as for any man, Jesus Christ is and must be everything—only after that does Father Arrupe agree to speak more personally of himself and narrate memories of his family and of his life as a student or aspects of his daily activity as Superior General of the Society of Jesus.

I was "steered off course" more than once. I proposed a route of which I had foreseen all the stages, but often we made other stops and turned into other pathways.

For example, I once asked Father Arrupe how he organized his days in the Society's Curia. I knew the tasks he had to face daily, the consideration he gave to every letter, every document, every visitor, whether a Jesuit or not. I also knew the care he took to prepare for each meeting and each one of his "interventions." I had noted that often he knew about the important world events well before me in the morning. I had also noted that, when I arrived for our interviews, not one dossier cluttered his desk. Before him was only one sheet of paper on which he had jotted—when?—a few notes concerning the subject we were to discuss, and also some difficult French words (because he insisted on using the French language, since he was addressing in this interview Frenchmen through the intermediary of a Frenchman).[1] In short, Father Arrupe's schedule was for me an enigma that I wanted to solve. Though extremely varied and demanding, it never kept him from welcoming people warmly. The answer to my question was not immediate, but came to me a few days later in the form of a note written by Father Arrupe himself. In it he said he was certainly going to disappoint my expectations as a journalist and as a columnist, but that having considered how he organized his use of time, one fixed point of reference came to his mind: The Eucharist is the central point of a day, and it is only in relation to the Eucharist that the true problems are posed and resolved. His "manner of proceeding" (a typical Ignatian expression which he often uses) depended on that privileged rendezvous with the mystery of the Son of God Incarnate. That was the reason he called the modest oratory next to his office his "cathedral." While celebrating Mass daily, he joined all of creation gathered around his Savior, and, through liturgical texts, he asked only to be the faithful servant for the greatest possible glory of God in the work and meetings of the day ahead.

In the course of our interviews, I shall refer to this observation in order to make the applications more concrete. It will be clear why the most eminent management experts, who had been called to the Jesuit Curia a few years ago to improve its efficiency, finally admitted failure. After some reading of the *Constitutions* of St. Ignatius and some listening to Father Arrupe, they concluded that the best solutions had already been enacted at a level which surpassed their competence.

Sometimes, after we had too hastily gone through certain parts of the interview, often the most personal ones, I found it necessary to ask Father Arrupe to backtrack. He obliged gladly, puzzled, however, why anyone would be interested in his literary or musical

---

1 At that time the French public knew Father Arrupe only through a few texts (those published in *L'espérance ne trompe pas* [Editions du Centurion, 1982]) and through the image of him projected by the communications media in their own characteristic manner.

tastes, or in some anecdotes that, to his surprise, provoked outbursts of laughter. Take, for example, the airplane incident in which a Latin-American industrialist had spoken to him of the Jesuits, of the esteem he had for them, and of the points on which one might reproach them. Glad to find such an attentive priest, and without wondering about his identity, he invited Father Arrupe to take a drink at the bar in the back of the plane. What a surprise it was when he discovered from the speeches of welcome which Father Arrupe received at the airport, that he had been speaking to none other than the Superior General of the Society of Jesus! Such situations—there are other examples—amused Father Arrupe very much; with no malice, he can see the humor in such misunderstandings.

Without that sense of humor of Father Arrupe, would the interviews, which are the subject of this book, be possible? Because the situation was unusual, not provided for by the *Constitutions,* the Decrees, and the Rules of our Order. First of all, he will remind you himself that we have an aversion to personality cults and we avoid publicity. Then, when a Jesuit presents himself to the Superior General, it is certainly not to ask him to relate his memories into a recorder, or to recall, for hours on end, the various stages and orientations of his spiritual life. The government of the Society produces a different type of dialogue, just as trusting, but more directly related to matters at hand.

Father Arrupe did not fail, at the beginning of each of our meetings, to create a happy and straightforward atmosphere, typical of the way he receives people, but in this instance all the more necessary because this lengthy interview of a Father General took place under the gaze—meditative or questioning?—of St. Ignatius, facing the armchair where his twenty-seventh successor usually sits. Even though it is only a picture, this "presence" of the Founder is sometimes awesome. Just as awesome, in another way, but still Ignatian, is, opposite the picture, the photograph of the earth taken from the moon; one cannot help thinking of the meditation that begins the Second Week of the *Spiritual Exercises:* "to see, . . . to hear, . . . to look at what the people on the face of the earth are doing: they strike, they kill, they go down into hell, and so on."

Nor can one help wondering: What are the Jesuits doing, in their following St. Ignatius, for the greater glory of God and the salvation of souls?

Such an environment, that of his office, made us very conscious that we would have to speak with seriousness about the apostolic tasks of the Society in the Church and in the world of today. But it was necessary first that we begin our journey together, to find ourselves as companions, so that I might be able to follow Father Arrupe on the voyage that I was asking him to undertake, in time and space. The way will be long, sometimes difficult; we might as well begin each stage of the trip in a good frame of mind. "What a thankless job I am giving you," said he many times, as he welcomed me; "there are really more interesting subjects than my life and my poor thoughts!" Or else: "Ah! You are again going to pose questions whose answers you already know—and even more!" The unassuming touch was there, and we could proceed.

Another typical characteristic of Father Arrupe during these interviews was the manner in which he often sought to transform the interview into a dialogue. "This is how I see things," he used to say "and you?" He then settled back into his armchair, clasped his hands in front of his face, and waited. He was not seeking in this manner a respite, because he kept listening closely, making comments, and asking to come back to this or that point in the text—"our" book, as he called it. But this "our," as I discovered gradually, was not a "plural of majesty," but a mark of sharing and companionship which he lived in all trust and humility.

At the beginning of this introduction, the question came up whether a Jesuit was the one best suited to conduct this interview. A more pertinent question comes up now: Have I been the kind of Jesuit, the kind of companion that Father Arrupe wished to have at his side?

For this is indeed the meaning he gave this undertaking and the reason for which he consented to devote so much time to it. He desired to relive in a Jesuit atmosphere, and not for personal satisfaction, a period in contemporary religious history, in order to show why and how, for a son of St. Ignatius involved in the service of the Church and the Sovereign Pontiff, "Jesus Christ is everything," and to invite all people to accept this truth, today more than ever.

Jean-Claude Dietsch, S.J.

Chapter 2

A ZIGZAGGED JOURNEY

JEAN-CLAUDE DIETSCH——*Father, even before your election as Superior General of the Society of Jesus, you spoke of your life as a "zigzagged path." What did you mean by that?*

PEDRO ARRUPE——I think I can clarify that expression by mentioning some of the cities in which I had very moving experiences, experiences that have made me what I am today: Madrid, Lourdes, Loyola, Valkenburg, Vienna, Cleveland, New York, Tokyo, Hiroshima, and others. Consider also that the Society prepared me to be a professor of moral theology and I became a missionary in Japan.

—— *It seems that you had very early the conviction that you would one day go to Japan.*

—— It goes back to my first year in the juniorate, that period when we do our classical studies. During my annual eight-day retreat, I had a clear "vision" that my vocation was to be a missionary and that it would lead me to Japan. And don't ask me what "vision" means: It's a question of an intimate experience that no word can describe and that can only be understood as it unfolds in time.

—— *All right, let's skip over the "vision." But what about this conviction — did you hold on to it in spite of all the zigzags imposed on you by the situation in Europe (the expulsion of the Jesuits from Spain, and then the Spanish Civil War), and by the direction of your religious superiors (the extensive studies in the field of medical morality)?*

—— Of course! But I must make a very important remark here: every moment of my formation in the fields of medicine and psychiatry was, in spite of appearances, a step that prepared me for my activities in Japan. I am really convinced that if, from the very beginning of my life in the Society, my studies had been oriented towards the Japanese Mission, I would not have received a better formation for this work than the one I received in preparation for teaching in the field of medical morality. For example, during that period I learned German and English (two essential languages in a mission that was first entrusted to Germany before becoming international), I became friends with a number of Jesuits who would later be my companions in Japan, and the medical knowledge which I acquired at that time would become of utmost service to me after the explosion of the atomic bomb in Hiroshima.

—— *Finally, when, how, and why was your desire to go to Japan realized?*

—— Before answering that question, I would like to return to what happened during my juniorate. After the retreat I spoke of, I wrote to the Superior General, who was then the Reverend Father Ledochowski, to let him know my desire to be a missionary. I received — after quite a wait — a laconic reply that made no pronouncement about the future. The next year I wrote the same letter and got the same reply which put off until tomorrow a decision I had hoped would be made immediately.

—— *If today you were to receive a letter from a young Jesuit who asked you to go to a part of the world equivalent to "your" Japan, what would you answer?*

—— Oh, I receive many letters like that! And I answer like Father Ledochowski: No, you must wait. You see, this enthusiasm to be a missionary must be tested.

Of course, when I received the second letter from Father Ledochowski, I was very disappointed. The rector of the house at Loyola, where I was at the time, noticed without much difficulty that something was wrong, because I was not very good at hiding my disappointment.

—— "What is the matter with you?"

"Look, Father," and I handed him the letter. His rather prophetic response was for me like a theme song that resounded in my soul for ten years: "Don't worry, Perico, you will go to Japan."

—— *And ten years later?*

—— In 1938, I was making in Cleveland what we call the tertianship—which is a period of spiritual deepening following the period of studies. Father McMenamy, who was our instructor, had to go to Rome to take part in the Society's Congregation of Procurators, and I asked him to speak to Father General about sending me to Japan. After an absence of two months, he returned on June 6 at eight o'clock in the evening. I slept very little that night; I had an appointment with the tertianmaster at nine o'clock in the morning and I couldn't contain myself. At eight o'clock Father Minister called me: "A letter for you. You are a very important person. A letter for you from Father General." I tore open the envelope: "After having considered the matter before the Lord and having spoken of it with your provincial, I destine you for the Mission in Japan."

Later when I was in the tertianmaster's office, I asked him as subtly as possible if he knew anything about my future. "Nothing," he answered. "It seems that your provincial brought up some difficulties and Father General made no decision. I then showed him the letter I had just received.

—— *One can see better what you called "a zigzagged path." But before we follow you to Japan, could you perhaps state more exactly the nature of your research in medicine and psychiatry.*

—— In the course of my theological studies I became interested in questions of ethics, especially medical morality. I had studied under the direction of Father Hürth, a world-renowned authority in the field. Then in my third year of theology I was chosen to participate in an international congress on eugenics which took place in Vienna, Austria. That was in 1936.

This was for me an unforgettable experience. I was not yet a priest and I had not finished the medical studies which I had begun before

15

my entrance into the Society. I was scheduled to read two papers. Before me was a very select audience of men of outstanding ability such as Niedermayer, Gemelli, Bibot, Allers, Carp, and the like.

My papers were well received by my distinguished audience. But I must say that I have never felt so small. Faced with the applause, I knew not where to put myself; and the congratulations I received seemed to me to be a joke. This success did not belong to me.

—— *It is, therefore, in part because of this "confirmation" that your Provincial sent you to the United States to specialize in psychiatry.*

—— I had begun with Father Hürth a very interesting work, the one which led me to the Congress in Vienna. This work had in fact two orientations: one, more moral, concerned "euphonic castration" such as was practiced several centuries ago; and the other, which depended more on mathematical calculations, concerned the influence of sterilization on the race. Don't forget that we were in Germany, at the time when Nazism was at its peak.

It was some time after the Congress in Vienna that I received a telegram from my provincial: "Plan immediately a trip to the United States"——signature and nothing more.

I remember that this task was hardly easy. At the time the Olympic Games were ending and the United States had sent many of its citizens to Europe for this pagan pilgrimage. But, having finally obtained a reservation, I set out, perhaps not with the poetic enthusiasm of a Christopher Columbus, but nonetheless with the firm decision to explore this new land which my superiors were giving me to discover. Upon arriving in the United States, I contacted Father Thomas Verner Moore, who later became a Carthusian in Miraflores and who was then a professor of great reputation at the Catholic University in Washington. We drew up a plan for the studies leading to my specialization. I should call to mind here that I had at my disposal at that time all the documented research that Father Agostino Gemelli had given to me, since he was of the opinion that he would no longer be able to continue his work in the open and that I was, because of my youth, in a position to use all the data he had collected. Do you realize what a vast apostolic field was opening before me, who felt once again like a "little boy" in the company of these great masters? In the eyes of everyone I had "made it," and as for me, faced with a task to accomplish, I forgot Japan!

—— *Then why, during your tertianship, did you again ask Father General to send you to Japan?*

—— Because when I presented my plans to the Provincial of the New York Province, he said: "Psychiatry? No, never. Every Jesuit who wants to study psychiatry needs a psychiatrist himself." I think he made that statement because a member of his province had just left the Society after completing his studies in psychiatry. In any case, I found myself with no plans, that is to say, available. That I took to be a sign of Divine Providence.

Let me add here that there are today very good psychiatrists in the Society. Recently, here in Rome, I met with a group of them who had come from the United States.

Chapter 3

_____

THE IMPORTANT WAY STATIONS

JEAN-CLAUDE DIETSCH——_We have seen how circumstances—but you yourself have just called them Divine Providence—have made your life, before your departure for Japan, a zigzag journey. Now, drawing back and taking a bird's-eye view, I would like to ask you this: What were the important moments, the major turning points of your life as you see them today?_

PEDRO ARRUPE——First come Lourdes and the birth of my vocation.

—— _Why Lourdes?_

—— For me Lourdes is the city of miracles. I stayed there for some three months. Being a medical student, I obtained permission to observe the work of the Office of Verification. I was, thus, the witness of three miraculous cures from the very moment they took place in the midst of the faithful who were praying to the Virgin Mary, and then on through the medical verification that was carried out by doctors who were atheists. This impressed me very much, because I had often heard my professors in Madrid, who also were atheists, speak of the "superstitions of Lourdes."

There was born my vocation, in that atmosphere of both simplicity and grandeur at the feet of the Virgin Mary, midst the noisy insistent prayer of the pilgrims and the sweet murmurings of the river Gave.

The next major moment was at Vienna — yes, at the congress of which we have spoken.

—— _Apart from your experience as a young Jesuit faced with_

18

such learned interlocutors, what conclusions do you draw today from your experience at that Congress?

—— Certainly the importance of scientific work and its influence. One can treat theological questions with great scholars only if one has first acquired a maximum of knowledge in their fields. It is because of this that I considered myself so ill prepared.

—— *At this period the Nazi Party was ruling Germany?*

—— Yes. Who does not remember Alfred Delp, who became a martyr? I did my theological studies with him, and we lived through some terrible times together. As for me who had come from Spain by way of Belgium and Holland, meeting with the Nazi mentality was a great culture shock. But I must tell you that it was essentially a *culture* shock; I was not interested in political matters.

—— *You didn't read the newspapers?*

—— Very little. I see that I surprise you! But you must remember that a young Jesuit in those days did not have at his disposal all the sources of information that you have today. And besides I was less interested in the news events than I was in the way people around me reacted to them. I used to like to ask others to tell me what was in the newspapers and listen to their account of it. This was for them the subject of friendly teasing: "Look! Don Pedro has decided to come down from his planet!"

Next in my memory come two events that happened close together: my ordination to the priesthood, June 30, 1936, and my departure for the United States.

A year later, an unexpected stay in Mexico was another important experience.

—— *Why unexpected?*

—— After the end of my theological studies, I was a bit tired, and I was sent for a rest to a small parish in San Antonio, Texas. A Mexican Jesuit, Father Martinez, whom I met for the first time, was passing through there. He told me that a true rest presupposed a complete change of surroundings, and he invited me to come with him to Mexico. The fact that I had no passport didn't bother him (he had many connections), and so I went with him.

During my stay there, I was kept busy with five hundred small Spaniards whom the government of Madrid had sent to Mexico for their "education." The question of "rest" put aside, this time is very important to me because it was a moving human experience to be with these children at a time of persecution. (Lázaro Cárdenas was president then.)

Afterwards there was, of course, my tertianship in Cleveland, Ohio, and my appointment to Japan. And, before my departure, the three months during which I visited Spanish-speaking prisoners in a New York prison. I made there some acquaintances that I cannot forget. The guards feared for my life when I went into the cells, for the men who were there were hardened criminals. However, I must say that, apart from some apprehension about the sort of dialogue I would be able to engage in, I never felt that I was in any danger. I was both witness to and confidant of remarkable cases of change and repentance. And on the day I announced to the inmates that I was leaving the United States, there was a sort of party during which we sang together, my weak voice joining with the powerful and deep voices of the friends I had made. It is impossible to express the mystery of the lives of these men, perpetrators of outrageous acts, and at the same time able in their own way to show a great deal of sensitivity and tactfulness.

—— *Finally you set out on September 30, 1938, from Seattle for Yokohama. After so long a wait, what were your feelings during your first months in Japan?*

—— I must say that, at the time, I did not focus on the trancendent aspect of the missionary experience but, rather, on certain negative personal aspects: the discovery of a reality different from what I expected and above all the feeling of loneliness. I began working with German priests in a country whose language I did not know. Yes, that is important; you feel yourself very much alone. And I experienced an even greater loneliness when I went to Ube, twenty-one hours by train from Tokyo, for my first mission assignment, although I spoke Japanese only very poorly.

Another important personal event was my imprisonment for one month in Yamaguchi. Japan was at war and I was suspected of espionage. That, however, I didn't learn until the very end. Without bed, without table, without anything except a sleeping mat, I spent days and nights in the December cold, entirely alone. I was tormented by the uncertainty of the reason for my imprisonment. Many were the things I learned during this time: the science of silence, of solitude, of severe and austere poverty, of inner dialogue with the "guest of my soul." I believe this was the most instructive month of my entire life.

—— *In 1942 you were named Master of Novices in Nagatsuka on the outskirts of Hiroshima. And it was there on August 6, 1945, that you witnessed the explosion of the atomic bomb. Several years later you wrote a book entitled* Yo viví la Bomba Atomica.[1] *Could you describe what impressed you most at that time?*

—— It was the first two weeks after the explosion that was the most significant part of the experience: the organization of our houses (for example, the transformation of the novitiate into a hospital, although we lacked everything), the working of charity in people (for example, the devotion of the religious sisters who worked with us), personal conversation with the stricken persons who remained dignified in their misfortune, and also the providential discovery of a sack of fifteen kilograms of boric acid, which permitted us, in a primitive way, to lessen the suffering caused by the burns and to save numerous lives.

But it was years later that I felt the keenest emotional experience. In Colombia I attended an American documentary film which faithfully described the morning of August 6, 1945, and its consequences. I saw in one hour the experience that had been mine for six months. I could scarcely stay in my seat. Everything that I had lived through day after day, minute by minute, was too concentrated in this film. Everything that I had endured in reality was too much for me to see represented on the screen.

1 Published in Mexico City. The passage in question is found in the French translation, *L'espérance ne trompe pas* (Paris: Le Centurion), in pages 197-223.

—— *You were named Superior of the vice-province of Japan in 1954.*

—— It was on the feast of St. Francis Xavier that the Superior who preceded me called me by telephone and asked me to come immediately to Tokyo to take his place. We had not yet received the letter of appointment signed by Father General, but he was faced with great difficulties and could no longer continue: calumnies, accusations of spying. We had problems with the police, with the press. These were very troubled times!

—— *It was as Provincial that you began your travels to speak about Japan?*

—— Oh, I began well before that, in 1949-1950. During that first trip I went around the globe one and a half times. Then there were other trips in 1954, 1957, 1961, journeys lasting six months. I have probably spoken about Hiroshima and Japan more than a thousand times.

I met, in the majority of cases, the utmost understanding and great generosity. But I also had some strange experiences. Among these, in a country which I shall not name, a very rich lady of high social standing invited me to come to her home after my talk. There in front of her friends and the members of the press, she gave me, in a formal fashion, an envelope. I opened it, not without impatience, on my way home; it contained the equivalent of only a few dollars. But in the newspapers the next day was the photograph of this "generous gesture."

—— *We come now to May 22, 1965, the date you were elected by the 31st General Congregation to be the twenty-seventh successor of St. Ignatius. In such a moment, what does a Jesuit who thus becomes Superior General of his Order feel?*

—— I said it in my first allocution by quoting a verse from Jeremiah, *"A, a, a. . . nescio loqui*—I do not know how to speak." I had no qualifications, and I found myself facing the Society, its great scholars, its great doctors, its great spiritual masters. Here was a little man who had parachuted in: What could he do? It was a moment of great confusion. My only assurance was, continuing to quote from Jeremiah: *"Ne timeas. . . . quia tecum ego sum*—Be not afraid,. . . for I am with you." Without the Lord we can do nothing.

Chapter 4

SUPERIOR GENERAL OF THE JESUITS

JEAN-CLAUDE DIETSCH——*However, before this "A, a, a," there was the Father Arrupe who was beginning his twelfth year as Provincial of Japan, and then later on there is the Superior General who decides, for example, to convoke another General Congregation in 1974-1975 (the 32nd Congregation, which has so deeply affected the lives of Jesuits today), and who in 1980 lets it be known that he plans to submit his resignation to the Society. We now need to move through this history; and I ought to ask you what were and what are your guiding principles, your criteria for discernment, your convictions.*

PEDRO ARRUPE——I think that we could even go back to the time when I was the Master of Novices in Japan. I was always very concerned that the true charisms of St. Ignatius be correctly interpreted. This is why I wrote five books on the *Exercises* at that time.

And then, during my last year as Provincial, I spent much time reflecting on and discussing with my confreres in Japan what we called the "limit situation" (*situation limite*) of the Society. We talked a great deal about it, and when I came to the 31st General Congregation I said to myself, "That is what we must do: show the Society the position that it has in today's world." My deep concern was: What ought the Society do? For changes were forcing themselves upon us.

Upon arriving at the Congregation, I explained to the fathers (I remember I wrote all of this on huge sheets of paper!) what the worldwide situation of the Society was at that time, and that some of the methods we used in the apostolate were no longer suited to life in the modern world.

—— *Your experience as Provincial prepared you to make this diagnosis.*

—— Consider—this is important—that Jesuits from some thirty nations were working in Japan. It was a small universe where we were receiving echos from nearly everywhere. This was the situation, thanks to my predecessor as Superior General, Father Janssens. He had made the Japanese Mission an international apostolic work.

During this time also, as I have said, I made numerous trips and I traversed most of Europe, North America, and Latin America.

—— *In view of all the experiences we have just recalled, and of the global vision of the Church and of the Society which you had at that time, we might reread some excerpts from one of your interventions at the 31st General Congregation soon after your election. It is a sort of platform, built little by little during the course of your past, by which you will guide your action as Superior General.*

> We see that the world of today and that of tomorrow tend toward a unity that is more and more narrow, and that a great number of phenomena increasingly assume universal aspects. We also see that our Society, as small as it is, has at hand relatively important resources, and that above all it has, from the very nature of its being, the possibility and the duty to act as a single body. Indeed, our vocation requires that we act in unity.
>
> According to our Institute, it is the Society, not the Jesuit as an individual, that undertakes the defense of the faith and makes itself useful to the Church. Our universalism does not consist in the fact that our members are occupied almost everywhere and in almost everything, but in the fact that we all collaborate in a more universal task, which requires a stricter unity. This is the very reason for our existence within the Church. We feel ourselves impelled to collaborate, led by the universality of the task itself. Therefore the collaboration will not be imposed on us from the outside; it will be, on the contrary, a requirement from within which prompts us to pursue a greater good, according to St. Ignatius' formula: "The more universal the good is, the more is it divine." For every province, collaboration will not be considered

as an evil to be endured, but as a good to be promoted with all one's might.

Before thinking of the action to be taken and of the tasks at hand, it is necessary to think about the problems to be resolved in all their complexity. Many of the problems we face today affect and concern all humanity. Therefore, the first question should be: Where do these kinds of problems occur? The second would be: By what apostolic action, by what means, can they be solved?

First, therefore, come the circumstances where the most universal problems come up, then the means of intervention.

I. The most universal problems appear in various classes.

    A. In the ideological order, they are, for example, atheism, Marxism, ecumenism, problems of social and international justice.

    B. In the order of culture: the cultural evolution of the West, of the East, of Africa; the progress and cultural evolution in human sciences and anthropological concepts.

    C. In the order more of politics, one notices phenomena such as the unification of Europe, of Africa, or other regions; the existence and action of such organizations as the UN, UNESCO, and the like; various groups such as the Common Market, the Association for the Defense of Civil Rights, and others. The objectives are easier to reach, the Council tells us, if the faithful themselves—and more so the Jesuits—are conscious of their responsibility as humans and as Christians, and make an effort, first in their own environment, to develop the spirit of cooperation on the international level (*Gaudium et Spes,* no. 89).

These facts should hold the attention of the Church and of the Society; the Church and the Society at its service owe it to themselves to be there.

II. *The instruments or the works and ministries* in the use of which we must not lose sight of universal aspects and criteria. For the solution of these problems, there will be need of a certain flexibility in apostolic action and in institutional activities. Examples are theological, philosophical, and scientific studies, and publications which are compelled to deal with the problems and to find solutions in the modern ideological context. The boundaries of provinces or of nations should not limit enterprises of this kind; they constitute

25

a universal work. In this case, the cooperation consists in coordinating the work and the people in a concerted effort on a higher level.

Studies and pedagogical methods must be restructured to fit modern exigencies and possibilities.

In this category are:

—— The apostolate of education in schools at all levels, which we must be responsible for and guide in the light of our principles;

—— the instruments of social communication, such as radio and television;

—— the social apostolate through doctrine and action in various centers;

—— action among lay people and mutual cooperation with them, for example in the apostolate of the press.

This glimpse is enough to make us understand that the existing structures, if taken too rigidly, would to a certain extent hamper the necessary evolution; I mean especially the "boundaries" which sometimes isolate the provinces. Hence arises the need to organize a common concerted action. All our members, but particularly the young—do they not feel we have to adapt in order to respond to new needs and show our leadership?

Adaptation must bear on the structures, works, men, and mentalities. This operation is not easy! Think of the transformation which, in the industrial world, they call "retooling."

It is something like changing devices or rearranging them to make us more apt to answer new needs. The procedure involves the following difficulty: The need is urgent; but if changes are hastily effected, prematurely or without enough consideration, they will result in disorder, waste of energy, and finally, disappointment and frustration with no real progress.

We must proceed in an organic manner. We do not want to put off the whole matter until later. We do not want to sit still, "waiting for the water to boil." But in all fairness to reality and to men, we should proceed with understanding of the situation and not without preparing the necessary resources.

—— *The program was laid out; to carry it out remained. How did you proceed thereafter?*

—— Above all I followed the Spirit. All the points which supported me did not come from me, but from the Spirit who has animated the life of the Church, during and after Vatican Council II. Take for example the letter on discernment[1] (December 25, 1971); a short letter of three pages, which was criticized—but I felt that therein a valid question was posed. Also what I wrote on Obedience and Service[2] (January 2, 1967), on poverty, witnessing, solidarity, and austerity[3] (April 14, 1968), on the four priorities for the spiritual renewal of the Society[4] (experience of God as an absolute in our lives, apostolic dynamism, the guarantees and progress of the spiritual life, and community life—June 24, 1971).

And then, in sequence, the convocation of the 32nd General Congregation.

—— *The importance of this decision and the spiritual context in which you made it appear clearly in your short opening speech.*

—— I would indeed say that, as far as I was concerned, I could agree that the decision to call a General Congregation has been the most important of my generalate.

I have never doubted, even for a moment, that God wanted the convocation of that Congregation. I had already understood this clearly beforehand in such a manner that all doubt, all possibility of doubt, had vanished from my soul (*Spiritual Exercises,* [175]). And, with time, this certitude became stronger. When subsequently I wanted to "consider through reflection" (*Spiritual Exercises,* [181]) the reasons for God's will, several appeared to me, which St. Ignatius enumerates in our *Constitutions* ([680]).

—— *So you do not hesitate to give an orientation and to make a decision which seem to you, before God and according to the Ignatian inspiration, necessary for the Society.*

—— I am indeed convinced that this does not come from me

1 [*Acta Romana Societatis Iesu* (hereafter abbreviated *ActRSJ*), XV (1971), 767-773. The notes in this chapter are supplied by the editor.]
2 Ibid., XV (1967), 23-32, especially 30-32.
3 Ibid., XV (1968), 276-295; also in English, entitled "On Poverty, Work, and Common Life," in Arrupe, *Challenge to Religious Life Today* (St. Louis and Anand, 1979, pp. 11-34.
4 *ActRSJ*, XV (1971), 732-740; English in *Challenge to Religious Life Today*, pp. 42-50.

alone, but concerns the welfare of the entire Society. That is also the case with my more recent letters on the Genuine Integration of the Spiritual Life and the Apostolate[5] (November 1, 1976), on Apostolic Availability[6] (October 19, 1977), and Inculturation[7] (May 14, 1978). It is the case, too, with my conferences on Our Manner of Proceeding[8] (January 18, 1979), on the Trinitarian Inspiration of the Ignatian Charism (February 8, 1980),[9] and the one entitled Rooted and Grounded in Love[10] (February 6, 1981). These are the dimensions of the charism of St. Ignatius which I am convinced we must stress today.

—— *I have reread these texts, not exactly like a member of the Society (if this is possible), but more in regard to their relation to this interview. That is, I asked myself two questions: For Father Arrupe himself, who is Jesus Christ? For him as the Superior General of the Society of Jesus, who is St. Ignatius the Founder?*

—— I have no idea what answers you got from these texts—for all that is a lot to take at one time.

A NOTE BY JEAN-CLAUDE DIETSCH

At this point in our interviews, a question was raised about the manner in which we should continue them. Father Arrupe would have preferred a comparison between what he had attempted to express in his writings, letters, and conferences and the characteristics which I personally had drawn from them. But if this were to become an effective procedure, the reader would have to have all the texts before him—something which it would not be realistic to suppose!

5 *ActRSJ*, XVI (1976), 953-962; also in *Challenge to Religious Life Today*, pp. 191-200.

6 *ActRSJ*, XVII (1977), 135-144; also in *Challenge to Religious Life Today*, pp. 227-238.

7 *ActRSJ*, XVII (1978), 256-263; also in *Other Apostolates Today* (St. Louis and Anand, 1981), pp. 171-181.

8 *ActRSJ*, XVII (1979), 691-7222.

9 *ActRSJ*, XVIII (1980), 115-163.

10 Printed below as chapter 17, pp. 105-160.

We finally decided on a way which is more in keeping with the spirit of our publisher's series, "Interviews." I had noticed the insistence with which Father Arrupe linked knowledge of Christ to the Eucharist, and also the very precise memory he had of the celebration of certain Masses. We realized that for him these were indeed fundamental personal experiences which would clarify his answer about Christ. Therefore we continued by taking these Masses as our starting point, as the next two chapters show.

Chapter 5

A LIFE CENTERED ON THE EUCHARIST

JEAN-CLAUDE DIETSCH——*When some young people asked you, "What can we do to know Jesus Christ better?" you responded by speaking much more about the Eucharist than about the gospel. Why?*

PEDRO ARRUPE——I could answer you by telling you that I was speaking to some young people who were members of a Eucharistic Movement!

But in reality I should affirm this fact: The Eucharist is the center of my life. I cannot imagine a day without the celebration of the Eucharistic Sacrifice. But it is evident that there is a relationship with the Gospels. We find in the Gospels a realistic, historical image of Jesus as he lived in Palestine. And in the Eucharist we find Jesus Christ living today among us. In neither case can we see him with our own eyes, but the story of the Gospels is the word of God. With strong impact it communicates to us the vital meaning of that word. By reading the Gospels we perceive this Jesus of two thousand years ago as living and very near to us. It is as if Jesus of Nazareth continues to live as he lived in former days. On the other hand, the Eucharist is the body and blood of Christ risen, living, present, although he is hidden under the appearances of bread and wine. He makes himself present, he speaks to us, he inspires us, and he gives us strength.

—— *I suppose that once again these statements are rooted in experiences you have had.*

—— Oh! Of course.

First there was one of the miracles I witnessed at Lourdes before my entrance into the Society. One day I was in the front area of the basilica with my sisters a few minutes before the procession of the Blessed Sacrament when a middle-aged lady passed in front of us, pushing a wheelchair. One of my sisters remarked, "Look at that poor boy in the wheelchair!" He was a young man about twenty whose body had been deformed by polio. His mother was reciting the rosary aloud, and from time to time she would sigh and say, "Holy Virgin, come to our aid." It was a truly moving sight which called to mind the sick begging Jesus: "Lord, cleanse me of this leprosy." She lost no time in reaching her place among those who were waiting for the bishop carrying the Blessed Sacrament to pass.

Then the moment came when the bishop was about to bless the young invalid with the Blessed Sacrament. The boy looked at the monstrance with the same faith that the young paralytic the Gospel speaks of must have had. When the bishop made the large sign of the cross with the Blessed Sacrament, the boy got up from his chair, completely cured, while the crowd shouted with joy: "It's a miracle, it's a miracle."

Thanks to my special permit, I was able to be present at the medical verifications that followed; the Lord had truly cured him. It is impossible to tell you what my feelings and the state of my soul were at that moment. I had just come from the Medical School of the University of Madrid, where so many unbelieving professors (some of them very famous people) and so many unbelieving fellow students always made fun of miracles, and now I had been the eyewitness of a true miracle. A miracle performed by Jesus Christ in the Eucharist, by that same Jesus who had cured during his lifetime so many paralytics and sick people. I experienced an immense joy. I had the impression of being near Jesus, and as I felt his all powerful strength, the world around me began to seem extremely small. I returned to Madrid; the books kept falling from my hands; those lessons, those experiments about which I was so excited before seemed then so empty. My fellow students asked me: "What's happening to you this year? You seem dazed!" Yes, I was dazed by the memory which upset me more each day; only the image of the Sacred Host raised in blessing and the paralyzed boy

31

jumping up from his chair remained fixed in my memory and in my heart. Three months later I entered the novitiate of the Society of Jesus at Loyola.

—— *The circumstances in which you celebrated one of your first Masses in Japan were rather unique.*

—— I remember indeed the Mass which I celebrated at the summit of the famous mountain Fujiyama at an altitude of more than 9,000 feet. I climbed it with one of my fellow Jesuits. In those days one had to make almost the entire climb on foot. One could go on horseback to only an altitude of about 3,000 feet. You had to get to the summit before four o'clock in the morning to be able to admire the superb panorama, because after six o'clock the summit would be completely covered with clouds and one could no longer see anything.

We arrived on time and we celebrated Mass in the most absolute solitude. I had arrived in Japan just a short time before, and I was still living with the first impressions which this new environment had stirred up in me. A thousand projects for the conversion of all of Japan were tumbling around in my mind; we had climbed Fujiyama in order to be able to offer to the Heavenly Father, on the highest elevation in all of Japan, the sacrifice of the spotless Lamb for the salvation of this great country. The ascent had been very tiring since we had to hurry to arrive on time. We thought several times about Abraham and Isaac climbing the mountain for the sacrifice. Arriving at the summit, the sunrise was magnificent; it raised our spirits and disposed us for the celebration of the Holy Sacrifice. I had never celebrated Mass in such surroundings. Above us the blue sky stretched out pure and majestic like the dome of an immense temple; below one saw all the people of Japan, then about eighty million people who did not know the Savior. Piercing the lofty dome of the material sky, my spirit rose to the throne of the Divine Majesty, to the throne of the Holy Trinity, and I seemed to see the heavenly Jerusalem, the Holy City; I seemed to see Jesus Christ accompanied by St. Francis Xavier, the first apostle to Japan, whose hair turned white in a few months because of the sufferings he had to endure. I too was faced with the same Japan as St. Francis Xavier, faced with a totally unknown future; if I had known then how much I would suffer, my hands would have trembled as I raised the Host.

—— *In view of that we can recall your first Mass after the explosion of the atomic bomb.*

—— The explosion took place on August 6. The following day, August 7, at five o'clock in the morning, before beginning to take care of the wounded and bury the dead, I celebrated Mass in the house. In the these very moments one feels closer to God, one feels more deeply the value of his aid. Actually the surroundings did not foster devotion for the celebration of the Mass. The chapel, half destroyed, was overflowing with the wounded, who were lying on the floor very near to one another, suffering terribly, twisted with pain. I began the Mass as best I could in the midst of that mass of humanity who hadn't the slightest idea what was going on at the altar: they were all pagans who had never attended a Mass before. I can never forget the terrible feeling I experienced when I turned toward them at the *Dominus Vobiscum* (we said Mass at that time with our back toward the congregation) and saw this sight from the altar. I could not move, I stayed there as if I were paralyzed, my arms outstretched, contemplating this human tragedy—human science and technological progress used to destroy the human race. They were all looking at me, eyes full of agony and despair as if they were waiting for some consolation to come from the altar. What a terrible scene! A few minutes later the One about whom John the Baptist said "There is one among you whom you do not recognize" (John 1:26) would descend on the altar.

I never before felt as I did at that moment the solitude of pagan obtuseness to Jesus Christ. Their Savior was there, the one who had given his life for them; but they "did not know who was among them" (see John 1:26). I was the only one who knew. A prayer for those who had had the savage cruelty to drop the atomic bomb came spontaneously to my lips: "Lord, pardon them for they know not what they do"; and for those lying helpless before me, twisted with pain: "Lord, give them the faith—that they may see; give them the strength to bear their pain." When I elevated the Host before those wounded and torn bodies, a cry rose in my heart: "My Lord and my God, have pity on these sheep who have no

33

shepherd" (Matt. 9:36). "That they might believe in you, Lord. Be mindful of them also that they may come to know you" (I Tim. 2:4).

Torrents of graces certainly poured forth from that Host and that altar. Six months later when, having been cared for, all had left our house (only two persons died), many among them had been baptized and all had learned that Christian charity knows how to understand, help, and give a consolation that surpasses all human comforting. This charity had communicated a serenity which helps one to smile in spite of pain and to forgive those who have caused us so much suffering.

From such Masses come living moments of sacramental intuition that cause us to understand things that are difficult or impossible to understand without faith, such as the value of suffering, the sublimity and the beauty of sacrifice inspired by charity.

—— *Since what you have just told me is so far removed from what the mass media often report concerning the "Black Pope," I would like you to give us another example, perhaps one you have experienced as Superior General.*

—— A few years ago I was visiting one of the Jesuit provinces in Latin America. I was invited to celebrate Mass in a local neighborhood, in a slum (*favela*) which was the poorest in the region, they tell me. About five thousand people were living there in the mud because this district was located in a low-lying area which flooded every time it rained.

I gladly accepted because I know from experience that we learn much when we visit the poor. We do a great deal of good for the poor, but they, on their part, teach us many things.

The Mass was held in a small open building which was in a very poor state of repair; there was no door, and the dogs and cats came in and went out freely. Mass began with hymns accompanied by a self-taught guitarist, and the result was marvelous. The words of the hymn went: "Loving is giving of oneself, forgetting oneself, while seeking what will make others happy"; and then it continued: "How beautiful it is to live in order to love, how great it is to have in order to give. Giving joy and happiness, giving of oneself—this

34

is love! If you love as you love yourself, and if you give yourself for others, you will see that there is no selfishness impossible to overcome. How beautiful it is to live in order to love."

Progressively as the hymn continued I felt a lump in my throat. I had to make a real effort to continue the Mass. These people seemed to possess nothing and yet they were ready to give of themselves to communicate joy and happiness.

At the consecration I elevated the Host and perceived in the absolute silence the joy of the Lord which is found among those who love him. As Jesus said: "He sent me to bring the good news to the poor" (Luke 4:18). "Happy are the poor in spirit" (Matt 5:3).

A bit later, while distributing Communion, I noticed big tears like pearls on many of these faces, which were dry, hard, baked by the sun; they recognized Jesus, who was their only consolation. My hands were trembling.

My homily was short. It was more of a dialogue; they told me things that one rarely hears in solemn discourses, very simple things, but at the same time profound and touchingly sublime. A little old woman said, "You are the Superior of the Fathers, aren't you? Well, sir, a thousand thanks, because your Jesuit priests brought us the great treasure we were lacking, what we needed most, Holy Mass." A young boy stated publicly, "Father, be assured that we are very grateful because the priests have taught us to love our enemies. A week ago I got out a knife to kill a guy whom I hated. But after listening to the priest explain the Gospel to us, I went out and bought an ice cream cone and gave it to my enemy."

When it was over, a big devil whose hang-dog look made me almost afraid said, "Come to my place. I have something to give you." I was undecided, I didn't know whether to accept or not, but the priest who was with me said, "Accept, Father, they are good people." I went to his place; his house was a hovel nearly on the point of collapsing. He had me sit down on a rickety old chair. From there I could see the sunset. The big man said to me, "Look, sir, how beautiful it is!" We sat in silence for several minutes. The sun disappeared. The man then said, "I didn't know how to thank you for all you have done for us. I have nothing to give you, but I thought you would like to see this sunset. You liked it, didn't you? Good evening." And then he shook my hand. As I walked away I thought, "I have seldom met such a kindhearted person." I was strolling along that lane when a poorly dressed woman came up to me; she kissed my hand, looked at me, and with a voice filled with emotion said, "Father, pray for me and my children. I was at that beautiful Mass you celebrated. I must hurry home. But I have nothing to give my children. Pray to the Lord for me; he's the one who must help us." And she disappeared running in the direction of her home.

Many indeed are the things I learned thanks to that Mass among the poor. What a contrast with the great gatherings of the powerful of this world.

Chapter 6

JESUS CHRIST IS EVERYTHING

JEAN-CLAUDE DIETSCH——*After these so rich and meaningful reminiscings, I return to my question: For you, who is Jesus Christ?*

PEDRO ARRUPE: That same question was asked me, unexpectedly, during an interview which I gave on Italian television about five years ago. The question took me by surprise, and I answered it in a completely spontaneous way: "For me Jesus Christ is everything." And today I am giving you the same answer with still more strength and clarity, "For me Jesus Christ is *everything.*" So, I would define what Jesus Christ represents in my life as *"everything."*

He was and he is my ideal from the moment of my entrance into the Society. He was and he continues to be my way; he was and he still is my strength. I don't think it is necessary to explain very much what that means. Take Jesus Christ from my life and everything would collapse—like a human body from which someone removed the skeleton, heart, and head.

—— *Don't you think that, even before you entered the Society, there were already some elements of this great ideal in your life?*

—— Of course, even if they were in a very embryonic form. Through the Eucharist and simple family devotions—especially devotion to the Sacred Heart—my father and mother cultivated the seed that the Society would develop later. Or better, that which the Sacred Heart himself planted, thanks to my parents, was cultivated later, thanks to the Society.

—— *The person of Jesus Christ is very complex. What aspects have impressed you the most?*

—— It is true that the person of Jesus Christ is, from one point of view, very complex or, if you will, it presents multiple aspects. But in reality it is very simple: Whether Jesus Christ appears as a weak, fragile child or as the all-powerful; whether he is being affectionate with the little children or severe with the Pharisees, all is unified and rooted in one single aspect which is that of love; it is there that the person of Christ has a perfect unity and its greatest depth. What was for me, from the novitiate on, a simple intuition is enriched daily and has become very fruitful. And the Heart of Christ as a symbol of this love has sustained me greatly in my life and has given me the key to understand the Lord without difficulty.

Thus, this love gives life to everything else. Jesus Christ is a friend to me, especially in the Eucharist. Mass and prayer before the tabernacle nourish my thoughts and my activities. This should explain to you why I am so deeply shocked with the ideas of those few who move away from the Mass and the Blessed Sacrament, and who try to justify this attitude by their theological stance. How I would like to see St. Ignatius listening to such nonsense! What a treasure those persons lose who do not understand what the Mass is, nor what it meant to St. Ignatius and to so many other Jesuits—great theologians or simple brothers—who entered deeply into his sacramental intuitions.

We must insist without ceasing on this fundamental truth: Jesus Christ is the Incarnate Word; he is the way to the Father; and for us Jesuits he is the answer to the prayer addressed by Ignatius to Mary in the chapel at La Storta near Rome, "that she place me with her Son." Such is also my continual prayer for the Society, "that Mary place us with her Son."

—— *I am aware that the Heart of Jesus, which has such a fundamental and constant place in your life, appears only rarely in your numerous letters, allocutions, and conferences during your term as Superior General.*

—— You are right.

From the time of my novitiate, I have always been convinced that in what we call "devotion to the Heart of Jesus" is contained a symbolic expression of the Ignatian spirit and an extraordinary effectiveness both for personal perfection and for a fruitful apostolate. I still have this conviction.

Thus, it may seem strange that, during my term as General, I have spoken relatively little on this theme. But there is a reason for this which we could term pastoral, especially with regard to the Society. Faced with the emotional reactions and aversions which manifested themselves a few years ago concerning even the expression "Sacred Heart," a phenomenon which had its origin, in part, in certain exaggerations and emotional manifestations, it seemed to me that it was necessary to allow some time to pass during which that emotional reaction—which, while understandable, was hardly rational—could disappear.

I had, and I still have, the firm belief that a spirituality of so great a worth, which uses a symbol (see Eph. 1:18) so universal and human and a word, "heart," which in language is considered to be an *Urwort* ("source word" or "key word"), will fairly soon find its place once again. We will succeed little by little in revitalizing the cult of the Heart of Jesus but without imposing it with an insistence which would only serve to aggravate or reawaken the reaction of rejection which occurred in the 'fifties and 'sixties.

It might seem to us that these kinds of symbols as expressions of our faith are suited only to poorly educated or even ignorant people. The words of Jesus tell us exactly the opposite: "I bless you, Father. . . for hiding these things from the learned and the clever, and revealing them to mere children" (Matt. 11:25; see also Luke 10:21). If we want to identify with the "mere children," the poor, the little ones, is this not an excellent way to imitate them and adopt their attitudes with regard to the Lord? "I assure you, unless you change and become like little children, you will not enter the kingdom of heaven" (Matt. 18:3). We could translate these words of Christ thus: "If you want, as individuals and as the Society, to enter into the treasures of the Kingdom and to help to build it up with an extraordinary efficacy, imitate the poor whom you want to serve. You say often that the poor have taught you more than books. Then learn also from them this obvious lesson: Love Jesus

Christ by entering through the gate of the simple love of his Heart."

In Japan I never hesitated to consecrate, at their request, a number of very modest households to the Sacred Heart. I knew and they knew that it was one of the best ways possible to approach God, the Father of all men.

★ ★ ★

A CONCLUDING NOTE BY JEAN-CLAUDE DIETSCH

In the interview which I have transcribed just above, held between Christmas of 1980 and Easter of 1981, Father Arrupe repeated the substance of what he had spoken in the concluding paragraphs of his conference "Rooted and Grounded in Love," which he gave in the Ignatian Center of Spirituality in the Jesuit Curia, Rome, on February 6, 1981. (It is reprinted below, pages 105-160).

I also desire to add this observation. Various dramatic circumstances cause some of his words to re-echo in a special way. On August 7, 1981, he suffered his cerebral stroke. Since then numerous friends of his, Jesuits and non-Jesuits alike, have been able to affirm to how great an extent friendship with the Lord, through the Eucharist and a constant devotion to the Heart of Christ, is an inexhaustible source of spiritual strength, of confidence, of humble acceptance, and of hope for this General— whom, in a manner at once respectful and affectionate, we call "Don Pedro."

How can we verbalize with what calm resignation Father Arrupe, who is perfectly lucid, is presently accepting these new dispositions of Divine Providence in his regard? Perhaps only by repeating the verses of Psalm 23: "The Lord is my shepherd, I shall not want. . . He leads me beside still waters; he restores my soul. . . . Even though I walk through a gloomy valley, I fear no evil, for you are with me. . . . Surely goodness and mercy follow me all the days of my life."

Chapter 7

A COMPANION OF JESUS

JEAN-CLAUDE DIETSCH——*To be a companion of Jesus—what does that mean today?*

PEDRO ARRUPE——First and foremost, it is to love Jesus Christ with all one's soul and, consequently, in a total and unconditional manner. Jesus Christ does not want half-hearted people among his companions ("friends in the Lord"). From that follows everything else: This companion, according to Ignatian terminology, is a person who, through love of Christ, is totally committed, under the standard of the cross, in the decisive struggle of our times for the faith and for the justice which that faith itself demands. There is no question, however, of a violent struggle, but of a commitment springing from love and charity. Thus the faith is "informed" by charity, and it manifests itself in works for mankind ("for souls," as St. Ignatius wrote). As for justice, there is no question of the kind which by coldness can degenerate into an "unjust justice" (*summum ius summa injuria*)—but of a justice well informed by charity, which is in reality a superior justice, a true justice which responds to the demands of love.

The companion of Jesus is, therefore, a man of service to the Church and to his neighbor; for him his neighbor is a brother. Philanthropy is not sufficient; it must become brotherly love—*philadelphía* (from *phílos*, love, and *adelphós*, brother).

—— *How does a Jesuit view this commitment to the following of Christ?*

—— In all of this: He realizes it through a "mission"; that is to say, he is "sent" by obedience, and it is exactly "because he is sent

41

on a mission that the Jesuit can be called the 'companion of Jesus'" (32nd General Congregation). He has received this mission directly from the Holy Father or from his superiors in the Society. But the Jesuit is not alone; he acts within a community, which is not really a monastic community but an apostolic community, one to be dispersed (*ad dispersionem*), extended throughout the world. Thus a Jesuit must sometimes live alone and meet his brothers only from time to time; but every Jesuit belongs to the "universal body of the Society," the only community of which St. Ignatius speaks.

Another characteristic is availability: He is always ready to hasten wherever obedience asks him to go. He understands the tension between, on the one hand, the incarnation and identification of himself in the situation in which he is carrying out his mission and, on the other hand, availability to leave at any given moment to go wherever he is sent.

The friend of Jesus is open and universal, because we are always at the disposition not only of the local churches but also of the universal Church. For this reason the heart of the companion of Jesus is open to the entire world; he senses himself to be a "citizen of the world" (McLuhan would say: a resident of the "global village").

For him, the model is the poor and persecuted Jesus. Therefore, he too desires to be poor and humble. St. Ignatius himself prayed for persecution for his sons.

Finally, I believe that the best response is that of the 32nd General Congregation (Decree 2, no. 31): "Today the Jesuit is a man whose mission is to consecrate himself completely to the service of the faith and to the promotion of justice, in a communion of life and work and sacrifice with the companions who have rallied around the same standard of the Cross and in fidelity to the Vicar of Christ, for the building up of a world at once more human and more divine."

The source of all this is the love of Christ, and the principle and foundation of the Society is, according to St. Ignatius, the fourth vow, that of fidelity to the Holy Father in all that concerns the missions; therefore, the heart of the Jesuit, subject to the "universal

Shepherd of the Church,'' ought to be open to the entire world. Our Lord Jesus Christ died on the cross and was resurrected for the salvation of all men.

—— *How do the sons of St. Ignatius encounter Christ?*

—— Your own answer would be more meaningful than mine! I believe I have already said what is most essential for me. You have the easier job of asking the questions, and I the much harder task of giving you answers in my own name and also, as superior general, answers which speak for the whole Society. A rather terrible task, isn't it? So you must interrupt me if you do not recognize yourself in what I am saying.

—— *Yes, and I'm going to interrupt you right away, as a devil's advocate (for there is a bit of a devil in me): Given the state of the world today, how can one say, according to St. Ignatius' aphorism, that the Jesuit ought to "find God in all things"?*

—— It is a fact that, according to that formulation of St. Ignatius, the Jesuit ought to find God in all things. Consequently, the question "How does the Jesuit find Jesus?" is very important, because this call to find him always should be rather natural to him, like air for the lungs and light for the eyes. In other words, something like that which is attributed to St. Ignatius, who felt a constant interior presence. The "in Him we live and move and have our being" consists in perceiving Jesus as a constant interior presence and, at the same time, in recognizing him in things, persons, and exterior events.

—— *But, in the long run, that happens through privileged experiences.*

—— Truly, in every life there are privileged moments in which this encounter with Jesus Christ is existentially more vivid and illuminates everything else.

For a Jesuit one special moment is when he receives his mission through obedience, a moment which makes him recognize this obedience as the express will of Jesus. Moreover, he will see Jesus Christ in the superior who sends him on the mission. That is one of the characteristics of Ignatian obedience, "to see the superior as taking the place of Christ."

The Eucharist is another privileged time of encounter with "the friend whom one awaits"—that moment of identification with Christ who offers himself to the Father and who is the food which satisfies the hunger of mankind.

Another moment of special importance for this discovery of God in all things, is to listen to his word in Holy Scripture and, at the same time so to speak, to discover the suffering and the cross of Christ under all their forms. It's a question of a special state of mind, acquired especially through the Spiritual Exercises. Often we set out to seek the Lord where we want him to be and not in the place where he is and awaits us. But, little by little, the Jesuit learns to recognize the Cross in its many varied forms, behind which the Lord is hidden. Perhaps today this is especially among the very poor, the persecuted, the scorned. One often hears Jesuits say that "they recognize Christ most easily and most deeply in the poor person who is suffering and oppressed." That, certainly, is a privileged place (and hence came "the preferential option for the poor" recommended by the 32nd General Congregation), largely because this experience communicates to us Christ through the events and reality of the world today, those events to which your question addresses itself. It is an experience lived and shared by those who are working in the slums of the large cities, in the shantytowns, in refugee camps, among the illiterate, and the like. This is an experience that has changed the lives of many Jesuits.

The encounter with Jesus Christ is an essential condition for the apostolic life of a Jesuit. The modalities depend on the circumstances, persons, temperaments, and occasions. It is an encounter that takes place sometimes in a way that is unconscious and hidden from the person who thinks he is not experiencing it. Notice the end of chapter 25 of the Gospel of St. Matthew.

—— *How do the Jesuits give witness to their friendship with Jesus and how do they share it?*

—— I am convinced that the witness that has credibility today is that of action, of living it out. The world—and especially youth—is saturated with words and speeches. It wants deeds. Thus the way to demonstrate that one is truly a "companion of Jesus" in the sense that we have been using is to show it in one's life, to manifest it in a transparent testimony understandable to everyone. I am referring to a manner of acting that no sermon could replace and that no unbeliever or tepid person could duplicate. It means living out the Gospel radically, without "gloss"; it means loving one's neighbor as Christ did, to the point of giving His life for him, that is, living in a detached way, as a poor person, and in the service of others.

This witness should be one of a life that makes sense only in the light of faith and which, at the same time, speaks to the people of our day. Today it is not sufficient to "live poorly"; poverty which demands "solidarity," "insertion," defense of those who suffer, and the like, is an apostolic activity which recognizes the equal rights of all, which involves itself with the most disadvantaged, which makes itself the "voice of those without a voice." It is thus that a "friend of Jesus" appears; he acts like Him, by making everyone feel the warmth of his affection and by living always at the disposition of others with a complete detachment.

All of this is an intuition, a truth, and a line of behavior which is deeply Ignatian. One has only to reread the life of our Founder.

—— *From listening to you and reading the texts you have written for Jesuits and for many other audiences, it appears that you have a specific acquaintance and a spontaneous familiarity with the thought of St. Ignatius—and not only because you are Basque as he was, or because you are today the Superior General of the Society of Jesus.*

—— Don't go and give people the impression that only the Superior General, be he Basque or not, knows the basic texts of the Society. Here in Rome, for example, I benefit from the collaboration of the eminent specialists who belong to the Historical Institute of the Society, to the Center for Ignatian Spirituality, to our archives, and to our university centers.

But perhaps I am a "connoisseur" (*fin connaiseur*), as you say in France when speaking of wines! To understand that, one must first remember that I made my novitiate in Loyola, and that I received much from our proximity to the "Santa Casa" in which

Ignatius lived and had his first spiritual experiences. I was very close, so to speak, to the vineyard from which we all sprang.

A decisive moment occurred at the time of our expulsion from Spain. The young Jesuits were leaving for Belgium and had two weeks to visit their families. I didn't go home; I took a room in a religious institution and for two weeks I studied the volume of the *Monumenta historica Societatis Iesu* (that collection of early texts of the Society) which treats of the *Spiritual Exercises.* I had taken it—I remember, without asking permission!—in the little baggage we were able to take with us for the exile. This period of reading, prayer, and reflection allowed me to enter deeply into the thought and spirituality of St. Ignatius.

—— *What important ideas did you draw from that experience?*

—— Above all, the conviction that in each era we must return to the original sources. We cannot depend on the charism of St. Ignatius merely in that form in which it was made manifest in the various periods of our history; rather, we must think it out anew each time, by going back to the beginnings, to the "pure idea" which is to be applied to the current situation. We must reincarnate this charism, not by rummaging through the centuries and the thoughts and deeds of the Jesuits during those centuries, but by seeking out anew St. Ignatius. And we should study him as founder, not as superior general.

—— *This is basically what you said in your conference on "Our Manner of Proceeding" in 1979.*[1]

—— Yes, I said that there is a distinction which we must carefully make. There is that which, for St. Ignatius, constitutes the essential charismatic elements, those which we could call the Society's specific identity; and with them too are the fundamental and common attitudes which flow from them logically and necessarily. We must carefully distinguish between these and the other complementary prescriptions which are much more subject to change.

We can no longer disregard the two levels between which the text St. Ignatius left us oscillates. There is Ignatius the Founder, and

1 *ActRSJ,* XVII (1979), 691-722.

there is Ignatius the General, who was the superior on the scene in one precise era, forming the motley community which constituted the Jesuits in Rome in the 1550's. To consider this text as a solid block to be taken as "the whole or nothing"—this is to ignore the most elementary principles about the spirit and the letter of the Ignatian legislation.

—— *Then doesn't history have anything to teach us?*

—— Tradition does indeed have its value. But societies evolve rapidly, and we find ourselves faced with new and very complex situations—"limit situations," as I called them at the 31st General Congregation—for which we have no solution. We must find one according to the charism of our Founder. The simple repetition of the past carries the risk of causing us to stray from this charism ·in the apostolic work which we have to do today.

—— *In Japan did you have to find solutions for totally new situations?*

—— Yes, and I also experienced the fact that it was not easy to make others who were thousands of kilometers away understand these situations! So the Jesuit Curia in Rome sent us a visitor charged with the task of evaluating firsthand the state of the Province and its apostolic works. As soon as he arrived, he called us together and explained his ideas about Japan to us. As we listened to him, we, who had been working in that country for several years, looked at one another—very, very surprised! Two years later, that wise and shrewd man had made our ideas his own, because he had understood, by living in our midst, what we were trying to accomplish.

—— *What was the situation in Japan?*

—— Japan had just gone through a very deep-seated crisis, and we had to keep this very carefully in mind in all our attitudes, actions, and words.

For this oriental country the Emperor was God and therefore invincible. Then suddenly came the unconditional surrender and the Emperor said, "I am not God." This was a complete material and spiritual rupture. And we, the foreign missionaries who previously did not recognize the Emperor as God (from whence came imprisonment, persecutions, and continual suspicions), we then defended the Emperor: "He is not God," we used to say to the Japanese, "but he is the representative of God, he holds the authority; you ought to follow him." For them this was something dramatic; and for us it was a delicate gospel proclamation. This was one of the principal reasons for my travels at that time: to explain to the entire world what the Japanese were living through and to seek aid and understanding for them. There was a new and complex situation, an extreme situation in which an entire civilization was hanging in the balance; that had to be a concern for all of mankind.

Chapter 8

A LOOK BACKWARD

JEAN-CLAUDE DIETSCH——*You have been, up to now, very discreet about your family, your childhood, and your life as a student before entering the society. You wanted to deal with other themes first.*

PEDRO ARRUPE——The reason is that, though those days—so long ago!—are important to me, I don't think they would be of interest to the reader.

—— *The reader would be surprised if we said nothing about them!*

—— All right, then, let's talk about them, a little. I am the last child and only boy of five children. My oldest sister is fourteen years older than I.

My family was very close, very quiet, and very patriarchal in the Catholic sense. I felt very happy in the family group. There were no major problems; we went to Mass together, and there was a feeling of complete trust among us.

My father was an architect. He built many houses in Bilbao and in the neighboring region. His character was very good, very kind. His temperament was that of a "doer." He had an outstanding tenor voice. When he sang in the chapel of a Jesuit college in a small neighboring village, all the old people in the area came to listen to him.

My mother was a very holy woman. I lost her when I was ten years old. She was scheduled for an operation, and the youngest children went to live with my married sister for a few weeks. When I returned, she had just died. Before taking me to see her for the last time, my father said, "Pedro, you lost a saintly mother. But remember always that you have another even holier Mother in heaven." These are perhaps trite words, but to me they are unforgettable.

Concerning my father, I can still remember that we had each year in Bilbao a procession in honor of the Sacred Heart, a very traditional procession. From the time I was three years old, I participated in it with my father, and for many years in the procession side by side were the tall Marcelino Arrupe carrying a large candle and tiny Pedro Arrupe, happy to be there carrying proudly his little candle. It was a well-known sight.

My father became ill while I was studying medicine in Madrid; I was then eighteen. When I arrived in Bilbao, he was already partially paralyzed. During those final days the procession of the Sacred Heart went by the house. I can never forget his look at that moment. It was a communion of memories, faith, and hope. For me it was very moving.

—— *There are people who would question you further about the connection between this event and your devotion to the Heart of Jesus. But you are not under "psychoanalysis" here. My last question will be more journalistic: In your family how did you live through the political situation in Spain at the time?*

—— On this point there is really very little to say. My father was not involved in politics. He was not even a journalist, contrary to what is often written. He was only one of the founders of *La Gaceta del Norte,* more because of religious conviction than by involvement in politics. He belonged to a group that made an eight-day retreat each year during Holy Week and which participated actively in the social apostolate.

No, sincerely, I don't see what else to tell you on this subject.

—— *Let's go on then to your student days in Madrid. What friends did you have? What groups did you associate with?*

—— First I lived for one year with my married sister. When my brother-in-law had to move from Madrid to Bilbao for business reasons, I moved to a student residence which had been founded by a militant Catholic. It was located in what was then the tallest building in Madrid—but what is seven stories today? There were forty of us occupying the top two floors. This group represented almost all the specializations, and its members came from all over Spain. Out of the forty, more than thirty received Holy Communion each day.

—— *Can you remember some of your friends from those days?*

—— Oh, of course! But, first of all, a reflection about the atmosphere of the group, which was most congenial. The seventh floor where I lived decided, after a year, to declare its independence. The question at hand was food. After checking the accounts of the house, we decided to do our own cooking. There were twenty-five of us. Happily, the mother of one of us came to our rescue! Oh, but what conversations and discussions we had! Really this was a very delightful time in my life.

—— *Was the friend who invited you to participate in the St. Vincent de Paul Society in this group?*

—— Yes, that was Pepe. He was the oldest of us; he was twenty-five and I was seventeen. He started a group, composed only of students, to visit the poor in, for example, Vallecas. This was for me a very new and different experience. My family was not among the very rich, but we lived quite comfortably. Now to be suddenly in contact with this poverty, this destitution! We began with some hesitation; we didn't know what to say to these people. It was very embarrassing.

—— *And who is this Enrique with whom you shared a special liking for "India," a pastry made with whipped cream and oriental ingredients?*

—— Enrique became a Jesuit; he's Father Chacón, the author of an enormous book on economics. He is quite well known in Spain. He is very talented in mathematics; he was always first in the class with a grade of twenty out of twenty. But in order to become a mining engineer, he had to memorize the Latin names for all the fossils, a truly impossible task for a mathematician! He began to get grades like 15 and 14, and he fell to second place in the class. "Oh la la!" he said to me; "if my father finds out about this, he's going to kill me!" "No, no, Enrique," I told him, "we're going to study together." After some time he came to see me, hugged me, and said, "You've saved my life; we got a 19.5!" Enrique also had a lot of trouble getting up in the morning; I had to threaten to pour a glass of water on his head to make him get out of bed.

—— *These students, then, were not those atheists who made fun of the miracles at Lourdes?*

—— No, those students were from the university. There were about five hundred of us in first-year medicine. I had a good relationship with them, too, and still have today with a few of them. I was even friends with a few of the professors. I liked my medical studies very much, and I can say that, after my family, the greatest sacrifice I made on entering the Society was giving up medicine. I had obtained diplomas in anatomy, therapeutics (with a special prize), and the like.

Still another memory is this. When one of my professors, a very distinguished professor but an atheist, found out that I was going to enter the Society of Jesus, he refused to put into his budget the scholarship that was in my branch of study. My friends began a small revolution and told him, "You must pay it!" He did, and later on, to my great and pleasant surprise, he came to see me in the novitiate to explain his action. He wanted to see me continue in the medical career and used this method to tempt me to turn away from my religious vocation.

—— *What were your tastes in the arts at that time?*

—— I liked the theater, music, and the opera very much. Ah, the opera! We were the cheering section, and we would go to buy our tickets at a bar where the plates were made of metal and the silverware was attached to the tables by little chains; you see the kind of place it was. We were young then.

At that time Miguel Fleta was making his debut. He had been a vegetable seller, leading his donkey through the streets of

Zaragosa, and he used to shout out his wares enthusiastically. As an opera singer he had a very powerful voice, but not yet very well trained. In Madrid he was a great success, and he was often interrupted by the enthusiasm of his admirers. He would beg the public on his knees to allow him to continue; and our group, we would applaud and cheer him even more.

I like *Aïda, Lohengrin, Thaïs, The Barber of Seville,* and also the *zarzuela Teresita* and many others that were popular at the time.

As for reading, I was not very interested in literature as such. I preferred scientific works on physics, chemistry, medicine, physiology, and especially works concerning the new chemistry for therapeutics (from whence came my special prize!).

—— *What do you think of the youth of today? I notice each time you meet them you easily establish a rapport.*

—— I don't have a recipe; it's more of an instinct. I am able to enter into the hearts of others, if I can say that. And that is St. Ignatius: to pay attention not to what they are saying, but to what they mean and what I want to say to them.

—— *I am thinking, among other meetings, of your address in Assisi on the Eucharist or of what you offered to the young Italians preparing in late 1980 for the meeting organized in Rome by Brother Roger of Taizé. There was immediate understanding although you were speaking of exacting subjects.*

—— One must speak clearly, sincerely: "This is what I think." Young people have a strong sense of intuition. They can sense when you are speaking to them with kindness, sincerity, and love, or when you are hiding something from them.

I like young people very much, because youth is the future. And I am convinced that, fundamentally, the young people of today are good.

—— *Many others don't share your opinion about the youth of today. They speak of drugs, false spirituality, marginal behavior, a rebel attitude. And you say that young people are good...*

—— ... and that we don't understand them. Thus we speak to

53

them in a way that doesn't get through to them. So young people go away and look elsewhere for something new because what we are saying to them just won't do.

—— *Why don't we understand them? Why this "gap"?*

—— Because we have the conviction, perhaps unconscious but nonetheless real, that we possess the truth. Therefore, to understand young people we must first of all listen to them, really listen to them—that is to say, without prejudice. They have other ways of acting, other attitudes, other symbols, other ways of expressing themselves, sometimes very vital. We don't understand them, and the young people sense that we don't understand them. Take, for example, the signs of respect. The young people present themselves, even before the Blessed Sacrament, in a way that shocks us. However, we cannot judge them by the standards of thirty years ago.

That leads young people to be in a class by themselves, united and radically challenging. Actively challenging in 1968, with their indictment of our social institutions and their ambitious aspirations. Passively challenging today, with their disillusionment, and we speak of it as apathy or indifference.

Therefore, whatever their modes of expression may be, the criticism that young people bring is authentic. We ought to pay attention to it. They are telling us that the civilization and the societies we have created are not satisfactory. Their idealism, sometimes impatient, is a proof of vitality and a source of hope. Much more than ever before, their generosity manifests itself in the form of service and, in the face of egoism everywhere, they know very well that man fulfills himself more by what he gives than by what he receives. They appreciate consistency between doctrine and witness of life, especially in what concerns the radical message of the gospel. They are sensitive to man and his fundamental rights, particularly in that which concerns the poor and the oppressed. By means of radio (the transistors!), televison, movies, and convenient modes of travel, they live in an atmosphere of information and universal interdependence; and they leap easily over boundaries—be they racial, geographic, political, social, or religious.

—— *Is that true also about the young Jesuits?*

—— Of course! Those who arrive in the novitiate belong to the youth of today, and they are the future evangelizers. We must welcome them, not in spite of what we consider to be their faults, but because of their positive qualities. It is our task to develop these qualities so that these young men may become true witnesses to the word in the world of today. Better than we, they will know how to take advantage of new opportunities and answer the questions of our contemporaries.

—— *What portrait would you draw of the young Jesuit today, especially in Europe?*

—— First of all, he should be, as St. Ignatius says, "over his childhood." He should have had the experiences that every good young Catholic has in normal surroundings: family life, student life, and the like, and even, perhaps, the experience of being in love with a young girl; that is one adolescent experience that, you may be sure, one cannot have in the Society!

In other respects, it is important that he be a man of commitment, who can take on a commitment to follow Jesus Christ for his entire life. And also he should be an idealistic man who has the desire to do something great for the Church and for the world. Finally, he is "a man for others."

Chapter 9

PREACHING THE GOSPEL TODAY

JEAN-CLAUDE DIETSCH——*How can we preach the gospel to the people of today's world, when new nations more and more confirmed in their own identity and in the uniqueness of their own culture are born and then develop? When ideologies clash in order to, in a way, divide the world? When evolution of technology is causing deep changes in mentality?*

PEDRO ARRUPE——This is the whole problem of inculturation. It is not confined, as your question makes clear, only to the countries or continents outside of the ancient Christian tradition.

—— *We will come back to this point. But first of all, how do you define "inculturation"?*

—— We find elements of this definition in the Apostolic Constitution *Gaudium et Spes* of Vatican II, in the Apostolic Exhortation *Evangelii Nuntiandi,* and in the final document of the 1977 Synod (the first official text addressed to the universal Church in which the word inculturation is used).

The definition that I proposed to the Society of Jesus in May, 1978,[1] is the following: Inculturation is the incarnation of the Christian life and message in a concrete cultural setting, in such a way that this Christian experience not only expresses itself by means of the elements proper to the culture in question (that would be only a superficial adaptation), but still further transforms itself

---

1 [In his letter "On Inculturation," in *ActRSJ,* XVII (1978), 256-263; also in *Other Apostolates Today* (Anand and St. Louis, 1981), pp. 171-181; see also ibid. pp. 183-184 for application of the ideas to India. Editor.]

into a principle of inspiration, at once a norm and a force for unification, which transforms and recreates that culture. Inculturation is thus a beginning of a new creation.

—— *Is this applicable to all people? and to all nations?*

—— It is evident that inculturation is indispensable, and that in a worldwide way. Until a few years ago one could think that it did not concern the countries of the Old World, with their cultures not only impregnated with Christianity, but even founded on Christianity. However, rapid changes have taken place in these countries, and the result is a permanent condition. This convinces us that today a constant and new inculturation of the faith is indispensable if we wish the gospel message to reach modern man and the new subcultural groups—the marginated, the refugees, the poor, the intellectuals, the scientists, the students, the artists. To affirm that these countries have no need of a re-inculturation of the faith would be a dangerous error.

I believe that the greatest obstacle to evangelization is the absence of inculturation, and that the greatest danger pursuing the nations of the Latin West is their unawareness of the need of this inculturation.

—— *How does the problem present itself on the theological plane?*

—— The Incarnation of the Son of God is the primary reason and perfect model for inculturation. Like him, and because he did it first, the Church incarnates herself into each culture, in the most vital and the most intimate possible way. She enriches herself from the values of each culture and brings to them the unique redemption of Christ—his message, and the sap which gives new life. None of these values may be suppressed or ignored; all must be encouraged and accepted.

This has immediate pastoral consequences. Inculturation supposes a new spirit and attitude in the Churches of the Old World, whether they are of the Latin or Oriental rites. It is a matter of renouncing a superiority complex and a monopoly on the forms of expression. For more than a century the world has ceased to bear the stamp of Europe (not to say the Mediterranean world). It is rapidly losing its Western identity. The number of nationalities, each of them with its own well-defined identity, has multiplied in a short period of time; and the opposite hemispheres are no longer the East and the West, but the North and the South. There is a clear and significant shifting of the centers of gravity on the planet.

—— *Along the path of inculturation numerous difficulties, even obstacles, arise because inculturation has to take upon itself many tensions. Would you, from your own point of view and in accordance with the apostolic experience of the Society, characterize some of these tensions?*

—— Allow me, first of all, to affirm this: If inculturation rests upon a reciprocal understanding, a true exchange, a sincere dialogue, the difficulties may be overcome.

However, let's look at the tensions which we must face. Some are theological in nature. There is, first of all, the tension between the universal and unchangeable values of the Christian message, which ought to be assimilated by each culture, and the contigent elements of particular cultures which, throughout the centuries, have imparted their image to Christianity. There is also the concern to safeguard each culture's proper identity; also the need to purify certain aspects of that culture which are anti-evangelical, or which prevent the integration of other superior values. Along this line, I would say that all "inculturation" demands—if I may express myself in this way—a "transculturation" (that is, an opening to and an exchange with other cultures); and this itself demands a partial "deculturation" (which includes a questioning of certain aspects of one's own culture). There is also the following tension: The riches of the Incarnation cannot all be contained in a single culture, nor even in the sum total of all the cultures of history. It is only the universal Church which is the authentic depository of the totality of revelation.

One can further cite the tension between the concept of unity (doctrinal, liturgical, and the like) about which we have struggled during the centuries (such as, in what concerns the Society of Jesus, the "quarrel over the Chinese rites") and the conviction that cultural adaptations are necessary to permit the introduction of the faith to each people. Inculturation engenders a certain type of diversity on a worldwide scale; but it ought to maintain union of hearts as a primary objective desired by Chirst.

Another group of tensions arises from the area of anthropology. First, there is the tension between human values, priorities in the Christian conception of the person, and the depersonalizing character of some cultures which subordinate the individual to the interests of the marketplace or of class. Another tension arises from the meeting between thousand-year-old civilizations and the too westernized, paternalistic, and self-sufficient presentation of the faith of Jesus Christ. From this comes the necessity of decolonizing the proclamation of the gospel when we are face to face with a nationalistic sentiment which exalts liberty and the possibility for each people to create its own future.

Finally, still other tensions are linked to the practical. Two things are essential, but not always easy to harmonize. On one hand, we have complex and profound interdisciplinary studies which seem to leave aside popular and nonscientific expressions and, on the other hand, we have intuition, which allows an approach which is more rapid and more of a piece with every day life, at least in appearance and in contrast with the studied approach of the Western type. Another practical tension is that which exists between the boldness necessary to realize great projects and the prudence necessary to avoid errors which can block the whole process. There is another tension also between the necessary fact that Christianity must become incarnate in order to be accepted and lived by men, and the certitude that, in spite of everything, salvation comes from God alone.

On this level of practice, too, I would mention the tension between the generations. The older generation acts with prudence in regard to all change, while the younger generation is always ready to burn the bridges.

—— *As for you, when you lived in Japan, you were aware of all these tensions, difficulties, and hopes—in other words, of the failures and promises of a dialogue which aims to be constructive within another civilization.*

—— Yes, especially when I was named instructor of the Japanese novices! For me the question was the following: How was a Spaniard going to train young Japanese Jesuits? I had to learn how to mix Oriental intuition and Western rationalization; how, without giving a course in scholastic philosophy, which contains too many untranslatable concepts, to share a little of the spirit of this philosophy which belongs to the Christian tradition. It was a complex but fundamental situation: No culture is perfect, and there ought to be a reciprocal enrichment.

—— *The 32nd General Congregation had confided a task to you, "the further development and promotion of this work [of inculturation] throughout the Society." And you responded in May of 1978 in the following manner: "I have accepted this task of the Congregation with all the greater interest because my personal experiences, before as well as after my election as General, have profoundly convinced me of the importance of this problem."[2] So, what were your experiences when you were in Japan?*

—— Oh! There are so many things to say that I would need another volume—which however, I have already partially written, in 1951-1952, while I was still in Nagatsuka. Let us limit ourselves to a few examples.

In Japan, for instance, the image of the Good shepherd is not usable, since there are neither flocks nor sheep. The same is true for the lily, which for us is a symbol of purity. It was necessary to find other symbols over there.

We have spoken of the paths of inculturation. Which paths was I to follow to reach the Japanese soul? The paths (*do*) of Zen. In other words, the manner of preparing and serving tea (*chado*), a ceremony which has nothing to do with our rules of politeness; the manner of shooting with a bow (*kyodo*), which is not a sport but a complete philosophy; the manner of arranging a bouquet of flowers (*kado*), which requires five years of study before one ob-

2 *ActRSJ*, XVII (1978), 256; *Other Apostolates Today*, p. 172.

tains a diploma; the manner of defending oneself (*judo*), which links elegance to efficiacy; fencing (*kenddo*), which is practiced as much with sticks as with swords, and which is as much an art as a confrontation. And finally (*shodo*), the way in which a poem is composed and written, not only as to the idea or the prosody, but also as to the design of the characters which express it.

I tried to learn all that, with reasonable success for a European, because I was dealing with an entirely new mentality and my task was to discover it. The result has only little value if one is not permeated by the atmosphere which corresponds to it. From the time of my initiation to archery, I served an apprenticeship which corresponds somewhat, I believe, to inculturation through Zen. During a time of intense concentration, it is necessary to identify oneself with the target at which one is aiming, in such a way that it is the target which attracts the arrow and that there is, then, no reason that the arrow will not hit the bull's-eye. It goes without saying that my first arrows landed far away from the target! And I often wonder what can come, in Western nations, from three-day "Zen sessions."

To sum up, I would say: If a man truly wishes to work with a people, he must understand the soul of that people.

—— *Isn't it hard to hold on to this period of initiation today, when we are face to face with the urgency of various apostolic appeals, and with the lack of laborers for the field?*

—— At the very minimum, it is necessary to acquire a certain mastery of the language, when one is in a foreign land, or of the ways to express oneself properly to a group. In like manner, one needs an adequate acquaintance with the basic elements of the new culture. If not, the apostolic work remains superficial and bears little fruit. Of course, if inculturation is necessary, it cannot be total. As a foreigner I too bring values which are useful. My own culture can enrich the other cultures. Nevertheless, to transmit these values, I must know the mentality of those to whom I am speaking.

We do not go to Africa or Latin America to convert these continents with European methods; we go there to serve Christ, the bishops, and the Christian communities—meanwhile knowing that we can also bring complementary human and spiritual values.

—— *How can the Jesuits belong to this body which the Society is, and also enter into cultural areas which are so different from one another?*

—— The unity of the Society is rooted in the spirit of its founder, St. Ignatius. This spirit, like the faith, ought then to be made incarnate in the different cultures. There are for all Jesuits common guideposts which are basic: "the glory of God," the love of Jesus Christ, humility, poverty, apostolic zeal, and so on. But what does poverty or community life mean according as we find ourselves, for example, in Europe or in India? We must apply the basic orientations to concrete situations, and then choose adapted apostolic means. We should take into account ways of thinking, philosophical categories, scales of values, symbols expressing beauty, respect, and the like.

Today unity is not expressed by uniformity of speech or dress. This unity is deeper; it is the union of minds and hearts. This brings us to know that we are brothers, members of the same family, in spite of exterior differences. An imposed uniformity, rather than variety, is what causes divisions. We are talking, then, of "colonialism." Why should all people in all nations speak, eat, and dress like Europeans? On the contrary, to give an example, allowing different cultural groups the possibility of having their own proper liturgy reinforces the ties with Rome, for the love of Holy Mother Church is deepened. The same is true for the Society.

Chapter 10

THE SOCIETY AS AN APOSTOLIC BODY

JEAN-CLAUDE DIETSCH——*The diversity of the situations in which the Jesuits find themselves—does that not pose a number of problems to the central government of the Society, especially when there is question of communicating general directives?*

PEDRO ARRUPE——It is evident that to write a letter to the entire Society (and I have written quite a few of them!) is never very easy. I must present the universal values—those which, precisely, nourish the union of minds and hearts—and accept the different concrete attitudes which will result from them. I must not impose on the Society something which may be only European. I must take into account the fact that throughout the world the vows of poverty and chastity, for example, are lived in diverse socio-cultural contexts. If, beginning from a common source, the plurality of applications is well made, according to the Ignatian criteria and in line with authentic faith and charity, then this plurality becomes the means of a union which is more profound, more true.

—— *In what manner does a Superior General, yourself in particular, maintain the Society as a body?*

—— I would say, first of all, that it is by means of prayer, because St. Ignatius tells us that the superior maintains the community spirit in his men by prayer. This is always the first Ignatian means for everything. But to turn to some means of action more in the line of practice, I believe the first to be utilized is to search deeply in the Ignatian charism—and to see to it that others do so too—since that is what makes us feel that we constitute a body, held together and inspired by this spirit. I have striven to encourage everything which can assist this process. Naturally, the Spiritual Exercises provide the most effective means, especially when they are personally directed, but also within a community. For, besides the work which the Exercises accomplish within the depths of each soul, they help to create a sense of the local body as well as of the universal body.

I have tried, especially these last years, to deepen my own understanding of this Ignatian spirit and, through letters, meetings, conferences, and the like, to communicate some thoughts which seem most useful for all. I consider knowledge of the Society's history very important; but it should be a history that helps us not only to know events—that in itself is indeed quite useful—but above all, to reflect on myself personally regarding the message which those events impart to me. This is a method extraordinarily effective.

Meetings of provincial and local superiors are also a very efficacious aid. First of all, because each superior ought to feel himself the animator of his community and then, in these meetings, this sense of being a body is had in a very special manner—and with still greater force if different countries are represented. To learn for oneself that persons of very different cultures feel, in less than two days, a harmony among themselves, with identical basic principles and with very similar experiences, gives one a great sense of the body of the Society.

—— *You said a little while ago, "especially these last years." Are there perhaps special current problems?*

—— At this time in our civil and religious history, consciousness of belonging to the whole body of the Society is very important. There is today an anti-institutional attitude which is prevalent in society, and which touches the Church as well as the Society of Jesus. As for the latter, a few of its members, happily not many, consider themselves as "detached" from the body. They do not have a strong consciousness of their identity with the others. They speak of the Society as something exterior to them, or more than that, as extraneous. They speak of themselves as Jesuits when it suits them, and not as members of the body when that suits them.

What irresponsibility! That is, I believe, one of the dimensions of secularization, a danger to which recent sovereign pontiffs have alerted us.

To foster this spirit of being part of a body (*L'esprit de corps*), it is essential that this body exist not merely in a juridical way (one can always discuss endlessly a point of law or take refuge in it), but in a supernatural way too; also, that it be accepted not in a half-imposed or a superficial way, but in such a manner that each one feels himself one of the members and identified with the body as a whole. In this condition, no Jesuit will be able to speak about the Society of Jesus as if he were an outsider, but as "we who are the Society."

—— *Does the Ignatian charism make the Society of Jesus necessary to the Church of today?*

—— Speaking generally, I do not believe that anyone could say that the Society is essential to the Church; for nothing in this world is essential unless it is of divine institution. Now, the Society is something human, even though born under divine inspiration and with the approbation of the Church. In fact, the Society was suppressed, and the history of the world and of the Church continued without it for many years.

Of course the Society of Jesus, being the fruit of the Ignatian charism, and having as its purpose "the service of God and the Church under the Roman Pontiff," forms by itself a valuable apostolic body; and I think that history testifies to the service it has rendered during more than four hundred years. Assuredly, during this time difficult periods have not been lacking, beginning with that of St. Ignatius. But, given the charism and service proper to the Society, these conflicts are humanly inevitable. Furthermore, the same history shows that, when faced with these conflicts, the Society always acted according to that spirit of service and submission; also, that in many ways the results of this attitude were positive for the Church as well as for the Society itself. Remember what happened with St. Ignatius himself, with Father Aquaviva, with Matteo Ricci and the question of the Chinese rites, with the suppression of the Society and what preceded and followed it, with the imprisonment and death of Father General Lorenzo Ricci at Castel Sant' Angelo.

—— *Could it perhaps be said that there has been a purification of the first charism?*

—— Yes, and also an enrichment. Today when the Society applies itself, in accordance with spirit and directives of Vatican Council II, to deepening the very charism received from St. Ignatius, it is discovering a whole cluster of treasures which are either new or which reveal various aspects which, up to now, were unnoticed or forgotten. This is making the Society into an apostolic body truly animated by values which are of great importance for the evangelization of the present world.

I have often repeated that if we were faithful to what the Holy Spirit teaches the Society about the different aspects of the Ignatian charism, we would be able to be more Ignatian today than in the time of St. Ignatius himself. That is to say, there is progress in our understanding of the diverse ramifications and meanings of some of his principles and his fundamental religious experiences. This progress leads us further in their applications than in his time (the sixteenth century), or in the intervening period up to Vatican Council II. The problem is that we ought to take into account what the Lord, our supreme head, causes us to discover—even if these new values often bring on us, as was the case for Ignatius, misunderstanding from opposite sources (from rightists and leftists, from progressive or traditional extremists). Was not Ignatius, on several occasions, brought before ecclesiastical tribunals as a man of questionable doctrine and accused of heresy?

It is certain that if the Society learns how to apply to present-day circumstances these new insights into the Ignatian charism, it will be able to give great aid and service to the Church. When I think about that, it seems to me that the Society could have been founded today and for today's world. No doubt our predecessors had the same feeling, because the Ignatian intuition, which is a profound and evangelical intuition, is able to and should adapt itself and be a source of great service in all ages.

In conclusion, I think that the Society, without ' being

"necessary," is able to bring some precious elements to the service of the Church.

—— *Are the* Spiritual Exercises[1] *of Saint Ignatius truly suitable for the present time?*

—— I believe that the *Exercises* have an extraordinary timeliness, through what they offer and through their impact toward changing the heart of a person. That is precisely what the world of today needs. The terrible human problems which agonize our contemporaries will not find solutions in laws or in reforms of structures unless the human hearts change beforehand. As a matter of fact, it is people who create the structures and the various economic systems. Consequently if people do not change interiorly, the new structures and new financial systems will be as bad or worse than the preceding ones. For this reason, the Exercises, which aim precisely at personal conversion and reform of one's life in accordance with the gospel, possess a peculiar strength for the building of a new world—a new world which would mean an integral and genuine human progress, and not a world in which mankind is a prisoner and victim of its own selfishness or of its inventions. It is against himself that technocratic and egoistical man transforms the world into a prison, and builds what is called the "city of mammon" in which there remains only, according to somebody's words, "the wind passing through." It has also been said that "a sound renovation springs from all the potentialities of mankind." The Exercises have this power of provoking a total response to the call of Christ from a person facing life's choices. The Exercises inspire true evaluation and true discernment of concrete human problems; and they display their greatest efficacy in action, with solutions which will be the best because they will be born of a balanced spirit which does not come under influences which could disturb it.

1 [We are using *Spiritual Exercises* (in italics) when the thought refers chiefly to St. Ignatius' book, and Spiritual Exercises (in roman) when the focus is chiefly on the activities within a retreat guided by the book. Since the book and the activities usually imply each other, the cases often overlap and the choice of usage must be rather arbitrary. Editor.]

The Exercises are not only an antidote against that so-called "future shock" which paralyzes and annihilates so many human forces today, but also a stimulant for the best energies of mankind. For the Exercises present the pure ideal of the gospel, personified by the figure of the God-man, with his message which is at once very simple and very sublime, carried to its ultimate consequences. And the Exercises do all this with a psychological presentation which is so human and so profound that they make this ideal irresistible.

Naturally, in order for them to be effective, they must be presented in all their purity; but they may be adapted to people and circumstances. Thus lay people can follow the complete Exercises according to the formulas we call "Personalized Exercises," or "Exercises in everyday life," or the like. In this, much progress has been made in France and Canada, among other countries, thanks to training courses and study courses for those who direct the retreatants.

———*Is there today a theology, a pastoral approach, or a catechesis which would be "Jesuit" properly so called?*

——— The answer depends, of course, on the meaning that is given to the expression "Jesuit" properly so called. For, I do not believe that the Society can insist upon a right of ownership in any of these domains. Since the Society is in the service of the Church, if it possesses something which might be distinctive, the Society will put it at the disposition of all, so that all may benefit from it.

Naturally, since the Society has an Ignatian spirituality, it will not be hard to find among Jesuits certain traits which are proper to them; for example, serious-mindedness and stick-to-itiveness in work, or fidelity to the Church. This latter trait may at times show itself through loyal criticisms—loyal, because they are expressed respectfully and discreetly to authority; but it should show itself especially in the deepening of one's knowledge of the doctrine of the Magisterium of the Church through new studies and research, and also in the search for arguments to defend it.

The orientation of study and teaching toward an evangelizing and pastoral application will also be a distinctive characteristic. In following St. Ignatius, the Society orients itself, through a life of prayer, toward apostolic action. And in our very studies, we are careful not to confine ourselves to "pure science," although that may be very useful and worthy of admiration. But the characteristic of the Society is rather to insert the problematic of the questions into life and to contribute to the improvement of human life, an improvement upon which philosophical and theological studies have such a great influence.

Today, one of the characteristics of our studies and pastoral work is that of adaption, of inculturation. That implies that a healthy and enriching pluralism be recognized, and that we know how to utilize the components of different cultures in order to enrich the doctrine and evangelical practice in diverse countries. From this point of view, a common denominator will be, with fidelity to the doctrine of the Church, the desire to do the research and experiments necessary to enrich the treasure of the Church. Such is certainly one of our characteristics. Research, experimentation, understanding vis-a-vis other values are the fruits of an opening which permits a positive assimilation within an Ignatian discernment.

While addressing the professors and students of the Gregorian University in Rome, His Holiness John Paul II strongly expressed this last-mentioned characteristic: "Do not be afraid in the face of the currents of contemporary thought. Recognize what is positive in their expectations and their efforts to advance the truth." And again, "I know that you pursue an open and courageous search for the truth, free of any prejudice and personal interest, with eyes fixed on the central mystery which is the Christ who works and manifests himself in his Church; who, also, has wished to place in the Church of Rome the visible sign of the unity of his Body, confiding to Peter and his successors the responsibility to guarantee the Catholic truth." For the professors he added, "Know how to be creative each day, not contenting yourselves easily with what has been useful in the past. Have the courage to explore, though with prudence, new paths" and thus accomplish "an authentic progress in the knowledge of divine truth."

Chapter 11

_____

THE TASKS TODAY FOR THE CHURCH
AND FOR THE SOCIETY

JEAN-CLAUDE DIETSCH——*Given the international dimensions of the Society of Jesus, you have a wide knowledge of how the Christian communities throughout the whole world are living today. What then, in your viewpoint, are the major problems today for the Church to which the Society ought to react by means of apostolic service?*

PEDRO ARRUPE——For the Church in general, the first problem is that of evangelization. In this sense, the Church is at the service of the world, and ought to bring God to it. But we must be aware that the world is not static, that it is constantly changing, and that, consequently, one of the conditions for this service is not only openness, but also reflection and discernment in order to understand the different currents of the present-day world. Concretely, it is a question of the interpretation and application of Vatican II, because this was the import and mission of that Council.

In this service the Church ought to be credible; that is, people must recognize it as an institution of great worth. We must avoid what is often heard today, "Jesus Christ, yes; the Church, no." We must avoid affording occasions for this misunderstanding, and work to make the Church well known in today's world.

—— *Is this distinction, "Jesus Christ, yes; the Church, no" widespread?*

—— Yes, particularly among the youth, among the young people who are committed, and even among those who seem to be good Christians. There were, and still are under diverse forms, the

70

"Jesus people," the "fans" of Jesus; there is a great admiration for Jesus, but the Church is not recognized. The Church ought to question itself about this misunderstanding. From this arises the necessity not only of openness, but also of dialogue. The Church needs to study the way of getting the message across. Language is not the only question here; it is also a matter of witness which can be recognized and understood by our contemporaries. It is a requisite that this life witness get across. This is the necessary first step to all discourse, to all discussion, to all dialogue.

Similarly, another very important problem is that of the relationship between *orthodoxy* and *orthopraxis*. It was taken up at the last Synod on the family. What does it mean? Even if doctrine is clearly presented, putting it into practice, carrying it out, remains difficult and demanding. So many people say they accept the doctrine, but they do not practice it in their life. Therefore, the problem for the Church is to present the doctrine correctly and at the same time to help people to form their conscience. It does not suffice to say: "That is the doctrine; now act according to your conscience"; it is also necessary to give principles to aid the conscience in its discernment. Perhaps in that there is a certain weakness on our part.

—— *Where does this weakness originate?*

—— Perhaps we lack a certain courage to speak the truth about what we believe. Perhaps we content ourselves with stating that if we think in one way, others think otherwise. Perhaps we hestitate, in a context which favors the plurality of opinions, to impose a point of view, guideposts, and references. But, for the development of the person, the concept of human liberty ought to take into account the doctrine of the Church as well as a certain number of objective norms. If not, the sense of sin, of responsibility, and so on, is effaced and even disappears.

—— *Doesn't this weakness also come from the fact that certain priests doubt their priestly identity?*

—— The situation has improved today, but it is true that a few years ago a certain identity crisis had spread among priests who were doubting the value of their priestly ministry, who were questioning their celibacy, who were hesitating about their relations to the hierarchy. Indeed, that situation does not produce the vigor necessary to present doctrine and to propose firm and clear guidance. The solution of the problems thus presented was and remains difficult and delicate, because objective data and subjective dimensions are closely linked. But this solution may proceed only in the direction of what the Church asks, and, for the Jesuits, of what the Society asks, for the accomplishment of the mission which has been confided to it.

—— *Another problem which confronts the Church today more than ever before is that of atheism and unbelief.*

—— We ought indeed to speak of this here, all the more because the special mission of confronting this problem has been confided to the Society.

On May 7, 1965, Pope Paul VI spoke to the assembled members of our Jesuit General Congregation XXXI on "the fearful danger of atheism threatening human society. Needless to say, it does not always show itself in the same manner, but advances and spreads under many forms... This is the atheism spreading today, openly or covertly, frequently masquerading as cultural, scientific, or social progress.

"It is the special characteristic of the Society of Jesus to be champion of the Church and holy religion in adversity. To it we give the charge of making a stout, united stand against atheism...

"You will carry out this task with greater readiness and enthusiasm if you keep in mind that this work in which you are now engaged and to which you will apply yourselves in the future with renewed vigor is not something arbitrarily taken up by you, but a task solemnly entrusted to you by the Church and by the Supreme Pontiff."

On December 3, 1974, the Pope was upholding this mission, and he characterized it "as the modern expression of your vow of obedience to the Pope."

Then during the audience granted me on January 3, 1980, John Paul II renewed this mission confided to the Society and asked it to accept the challenge "which has historical and eschatological dimensions"—such was the expression of the Holy Father.

Of John Paul II as of Paul VI, I asked, "What should we do?" Their response was the same, "You find the way!" Furthermore, given the universal breadth of the manifestation of atheism and the different forms of disbelief, I believe that the mission which has been assigned involves all the work of the Society. It is not the affair of a particular apostolate, reserved to a few specialists, but a dimension common to all the apostolic works of the Society. Numerous Jesuits are in contact with unbelievers or with people threatened by lack of belief even in apostolates which could be termed traditional. There is no need, for example, to leave a Jesuit university or college to meet unbelievers; they are found among those who have been our students for many years. The same phenomenon is present at many retreat houses; many retreat directors have unbelievers or doubters come to see them. The situation is not different for those who are in the parishes or those who work and live in the labor world. The apostolate of the prisons and hospitals affords an excellent occasion for contact with nonbelievers.

It is important to be aware of the diversity and extent of contemporary unbelief; state atheism, atheistic philosophical doctrines of varied nuances, then agnosticism which is no less serious-minded, and finally and much more frequent, simple nonbelief or indifference. It happens that people say they do not meet unbelief because they think only of atheism in the form of declared conviction or spelled-out doctrine; much more frequent, in reality, is unbelief or practical indifference.

—— *How does this last-mentioned unbelief manifest itself?*

—— It implies a judgment, at least implicit, that God is without meaning or importance, without relation to real life; consequently, the question of God isn't even raised. It is difficult not to meet this type. Frequently there is also the disbelief or "impossibility" of believing which is the fruit of scandal about the evil in the world, or about the deformed images of God which modern man instinctively rejects.

On the contrary, it is not necessary to consider as unbelievers those who, while not sharing our faith in Jesus Christ, nevertheless recognize God and give him a place in their heart and life. On the other hand, it is not unusual that, in countries that have been known for their Christianity, the difficulties concerning Christ, or even concerning the Church and its credibility, affect at the same time their very belief in God.

Thus another major aspect of the present situation is this. There is a close relation between the problems of unbelievers properly so called and the difficulties of belief which believers themselves often encounter. Sometimes there is an imperceptible transition from one to the other. Besides, the difficulties of belief are also in ourselves. And in recent times more than one Jesuit of any age has passed through a true crisis of faith. To be concerned with unbelief is not, therefore, to be concerned with and to address only the unbelievers properly so called in order to aid them, but also to be concerned with and address believers—including priests and religious—who are experiencing the difficulties of belief characteristic of the contemporary era.

In this respect, the Church and the Society make use of a specific means, the *Spiritual Exercises.* By means of them a person converts himself and forms himself in order to orient his life in accordance with the end for which he has been created.

In facing the different types of disbelief, the Exercises turn the attention to the fundamental point which is, according to a very Ignatian formula, the conversion of hearts. The first thing that all members of the Church, bishops as well as priests and lay people, expect from Jesuits is that they give the Exercises. This is the primordial task of the Society.

—— *But do we have only the Exercises?*

—— No, of course not! On December 3, 1974, Paul VI thus described the Society:

"Wherever in the Church, even in the most difficult and extreme fields, in the crossroads of ideologies, in the front line of social conflict, there has been and there is confrontation between the deepest desires of man and the perennial message of the gospel, there also there have been, and there are, Jesuits.''[1]

Thus, as "shock troops," we find ourselves in the front line; we are on the firing line. That supposes on our part a deep spiritual commitment, because there are risks. As a young priest who had made a mistake said to me a few years ago, "Father, I recognize my fault. But, you see, when you are fighting on the front line, it may happen that you find yourself surrounded by the enemy. When you see this, the important thing is to get back within your own lines." I find this is very revealing image.

Sometimes we have to intervene quickly, to answer questions on the radio or television, to write an article about a situation or a difficult problem without having too much time to prepare; then, certain of our phrases are poorly understood.

—— *And this happens within "our camp"?*

—— Oh, yes! Too often we judge another not according to what he thinks in *his* head, but according to what we think in ours. We remain very subjective. So we must understand another by first trying to put ourselves in his place. I do not wish here to defend the Society at any price, but something like that is indeed the source of many misunderstandings. Nevertheless, in all the domains where we are present, we cannot speak in terms of scholastic philosophy; we must utilize the language of the human sciences even to express theological concepts. Surely that involves some inaccuracies, but we must by all means find the language which presents the idea in a comprehensible way. If, today, I use terms like *formally, materially, sensus compositus, sensus divisus,* or the like, my questioner understands nothing. With a Marxist, it is necessary to use elements of the Marxist vocabulary to explain Christianity to him. As St. Ignatius said: "Enter through their door so they may exit through ours."

The Church is experiencing radical situations today—radical from the evangelical point of view to be sure!—on both the intellec-

1 [See *Documents of the 31st and 32nd General Congregations of the Society of Jesus* (St. Louis, 1977), p. 527. Editor.]

tual and social level. It is for this reason that we must put the intellectual tradition of the Society at its disposal, to confront these situations, and also to cooperate with the bishops in the formation of priests. But there is not only the intellectual domain. The Church asks us—and this is also in the spirituality of St. Ignatius as criteria for choice of apostolates—to go where others may not go or where there are too few; these are often difficult, complex situations which demand a great apostolic commitment in what concerns, for example, poverty.

We can also recall the importance of certain missions, like that of being in contact with the other great religions, and call to mind, for example, Matteo Ricci, whose four-hundredth anniversary of arrival in Chinese territory we are about to celebrate.

—— *Has there not been an evolution in the concept of mission?*

—— Yes, it is necessary to state. Today the difference between what was called in the past "foreign missions" and what is the general mission of the Church is blurred. We can no longer make distinctions; the criteria are universal. For evangelization, we must recognize the new paganism in the European countries, in the United States, and in many other places. The methods are almost the same.

It is a situation which also brings up this characteristic phenomenon: Nowadays priests are sent by the former "missionary countries" into countries of long-standing Christianity.

There are also the countries for which the Church asks the Jesuits, as well as other religious, to have a special apostolic concern: China (almost a thousand million people), the Communist countries of Eastern Europe (with their militant and even belligerent atheism), and the Islamic countries (these latter have great power of penetration, with an undeniable zeal and important financial support).

Then, there are the new problems which the present state of the world and the disintegration of societies pose; the problem, for example, of the refugees or the drug problem.

With respect to drugs, in 1980 during the Synod of Bishops on the family, I made an intervention. The drug problem constitutes, in fact, one of the factors most destructive of the essential values of the family unit. Because of it, relations based on sincerity and confidence which ought to exist among the members of a family are altered, too often ending in total lack of communication. How many young people are thus "isolated," no longer having any contact with their parents, and becoming easy prey for international traffickers.

—— *At Christmas, 1979, you sent a telegram to some twenty Major Superiors of the Society in different parts of the world. You asked them, "What can we do to help the refugees?"*

—— At that time, as a matter of fact, because of information that I was receiving, I was particularly upset by the situation of those who were called "the boat people," the refugees of the sea. The response of the Society was immediate and remarkable. Then in 1981, in order to coordinate the services which the Jesuits were able to supply according to their possibilities either in the so-called "relocation" camps or in the welcoming countries, I created, right here in our Roman Jesuit Curia, a "Jesuit Refugee Service." For one would not readily know how to conceive of greater needs, spiritual and material, than those of the approximately sixteen million refugees dispersed throughout the world today.

Facing these problems, the Jesuits ought to work in an Ignatian manner, that is, not to limit themselves to a task of assistance—which remains, by all means, necessary—but also to reflect on the root causes of these situations, on their meaning. The charism of the Society is to invest its forces in the theological, philosophical, and sociological fields in order to study the tragic manifestations of the misunderstandings which exist in the bosom of societies, as well as the disagreements among governments throughout the world, and that in view of bringing remedies there which are based on the gospel, on the word of God.

It is in this sense that, in the beginning of the summer of 1981, I am going to present to the general assembly of the Symposium of the Episcopal Conferences of Africa and Madagascar a report on the problem of refugees in Africa—a problem which constitutes for me an appeal and a challenge to the Church. This report studies the breadth and complexity of the problem of the refugees, in the perspective of an opportunity to give life in Africa to the ecclesiology of Vatican Council II.

Chapter 12

_____

THE APPROACH TO MARXISM

JEAN-CLAUDE DIETSCH——*Are the Jesuits able to collaborate with the Marxists toward solving the problems which face contemporary societies?*

PEDRO ARRUPE——It is important to distinguish Marxism from Marxists, the ideology from the people.

I can bring up here, first of all, my meetings with members of Marxist governments (such as Cuba, Hungary, Croatia). When I find myself in contact with men who defend institutionalized state Marxism, I think to myself that these are men who have a soul, whom Jesus Christ came to save, and whom I must win over to Jesus Christ. I cannot accept their Marxism, but at the same time I must speak to them, question them, make them think, open them to the possibility of the Church. It is a work of a pastoral nature, which is not primarily philosophical or theological. It is not possible to begin by repeating doctrine purely and simply; this is not pastoral.

I had experience with this for a long time with the youth in Japan. We would speak first about human questions, family questions, social problems, and so on. Little by little, we would speak of Jesus Christ as a man, not yet as God. Perhaps one day would come the moment of faith. It is the same thing when dealing with a Marxist; I am not going, as an opening play, to expose him to the doctrine of the Church and its position in regard to Marxism.

This pastoral approach is something very important to understand. It can be aided, among Christians, by a religious instruction which teaches how to discern values; it is along this line that I intervened in the Synod of Bishops in October 1977.

—— And in the field, if I may express myself in this manner?

—— According to the situations, different types of collaboration are possible and even desirable, because they promote personal contact. This collaboration may be called forth by concrete action. Thus, in Italy, Jesuits have collaborated with the Communists in the regions devastated by the recent earthquake. Another situation is: It happens that in a few countries under Marxist regimes, Jesuits' teach in state universities. This is collaboration that could no doubt be qualified as ambiguous, but I must remember that, in order to fulfill the mission assigned to the Society, we must be "in contact" and maintain the dialogue.

The situation in Central and South America is very complex too. Action for justice, defense of the most impoverished, the struggle for respect of the rights of man lead to working together. The decisions to be made there demand deep analysis and great discretion. What I wrote to the major superiors of these provinces of the Society in December 1980[1] is valid in other situations.

> 15. To adopt, therefore, not just some elements or some methodological insights, but Marxist analysis as a whole, is something we cannot accept....

> 19. [At the same time], as regards Marxists themselves, we should remain fraternally open to dialogue with them. However, true to the spirit of *Gaudium et Spes* (no. 21, paragraph 6), we ought not to refuse practical cooperation in concrete cases where the common good seems to call for it. Naturally, we must keep in mind our own special role as priests and religious, and never act like lone rangers in our dealings with the Christian community and its responsible leaders. We must ensure that any collaboration on our part is only concerned with activities acceptable to a Christian. In this whole area we have always the obligation to maintain our own identity; because we accept some points of view

1 [The letter On Marxist Analysis is in *ActRSJ,* XVIII (1980), 339-346. For similar ideas addressed to the Synod of Bishops in Rome on October 19, 1977, see Father Arrupe's *Justice with Faith Today* (Anand and St. Louis, 1980), pp. 253-258. Editor.]

that are valid, we should not allow ourselves to be carried as far as approval of the analysis in its totality; we must ever act in accordance with our faith and the principles of action that it inspires. So, let us behave in such a way that Christianity can be seen to be a message that has greater value for humankind than any concept, however useful, of Marxist analysis.

20. Finally, we should also firmly oppose the efforts of anyone who wishes to take advantage of our reservations about Marxist analysis in order to condemn as Marxist or Communist, or at least to minimize esteem for, a commitment to justice and the cause of the poor, the defense of their rights against those who exploit them, the urging of legitimate claims. Have we not often seen forms of anti-Communism that are nothing but means for concealing injustice? In this respect as well, let us remain true to ourselves and not permit anyone to exploit our critical assessment of Marxism and Marxist analysis.

Chapter 13

HOPE AND OPTIMISM

JEAN-CLAUDE DIETSCH——*You have been called an "optimist," and even an "incorrigible optimist"! What is the basis for this attitude of yours?—in a world whose structures, painfully rebuilt after the Second World War, seem once again to be seriously shaken.*

PEDRO ARRUPE——I am quite happy to be called an optimist, but my optimism is not of the utopian variety. It is based on hope. What is an optimist? I can answer for myself in a very simple fashion: He or she is a person who has the conviction that God knows, can do, and will do what is best for mankind. This conviction is based on faith and charity, because we believe that the Lord knows what is best for us, even though we ourselves do not know what it is; that he can do it because he is all-powerful; and that he will do it because he loves us. This is the basis of that confidence which is related to hope, although theologically distinct from it, and which renders this hope unshakeable.

What the world needs most today is hope. For in many areas the world is acquainted with great disillusionments. Some examples? Technology, which was formerly the bearer of hope, now causes fear. We are afraid because of the arms race; we are also afraid that the world will soon be run by machines, by computers. In the field of biology the concern comes from genetic research; are they going to produce monsters? In the field of politics, which ought to build up the city of man, are found radicalism and extremism of the right or of the left with, as consequences, terrorism, torture, and the like. Thus the foundations of hope have become the sources of fear.

And we find this also in the field of religion; men who claimed to have killed God now find that a world without God is impossible. And what they search for to regulate morality, social structures, and so on is, in fact, God. For they killed a God who did not exist, one whom they had fabricated in their own image. Today, disillusioned by the idols of this world, they are in search of the true God.

Teilhard de Chardin used to say, "The world will belong to the one who will give it the greatest hope." For us this is very important from an evangelical point of view; we must nurture this spirit of hope, this optimism about which we have just spoken.

In other words, "the future is in the hands of those who can give tomorrow's generations reasons to live and hope" (*Gaudium et Spes,* no. 31). It is interesting to note that, during Vatican Council II, the Council Fathers changed the [opening] words [of their pastoral constitution on The Church in the Modern World] from "The grief and anguish" (*Luctus et Angor*) to "The joy and the hope" (*Gaudium et Spes*). They saw in the latter wording the positive message which they wished to convey.

—— *You said that true optimism is not utopian?*

—— Yes, for all hope includes the element of risk, and there is a place for a discernment which takes human weakness into account. But one who has no hope because he fears risk flounders in despair; and one who hopes without being aware of the risk is rash. The risk is worth the while because of our faith in God.

I like to call Abraham to mind. "Hoping against hope, Abraham believed.... He never questioned or doubted God's promise; rather, he was strengthened in faith and gave glory to God, fully persuaded that God could do whatever he had promised" (Romans 4:18-22).

Another text which I like to call to mind is that about the "small remnant." It had no power but kept its confidence in God; and it kept alive the hope of the people of Israel. "Then the remnant of Jacob shall be in the midst of many peoples, like dew coming from the Lord, like showers upon the grass, which tarry not for men nor wait for the sons of men" (Micah 5:7).

It is necessary to note also that, contrary to utopian principles,

Christian hope begins now. It is not merely for the future. Although indeed eschatological, it exists already, in the present time. And its fullness is found in charity for all people. It has in our day a social dimension which is founded on the mutual love of all people for one another. It is what St. Paul said to the first communities, and it is what he gave witness to in his own life. He is an example for us.

It is on this foundation that I am an incorrigible optimist!

—— *That, you know, is a journalistic expression.*

—— Perhaps I am indeed incorrigible! But I owe this optimistic outlook first of all to the grace of God, and then to my experience of life.

In Lourdes, I acquired an awareness of the power of God as he intervenes in history.

In Marneffe, after our expulsion from Spain, I lived in a community of 350 persons who wondered each evening if they would have enough food for the following day. And each day, we had enough.

In the Yamaguchi prison, I was alone for thirty-five days, wondering why I was there, for how long, and if, in the end, I might be executed. When this "experience" was over, you could not help but believe in a special Providence.

And immediately after the explosion of the atomic bomb in Hiroshima—shouldn't I remember how we were able to feed and care for so many wounded?

When, in the following years, I traveled throughout the world seeking men and collecting funds for Japan, I was the witness to a rare generosity and to extraordinary sacrifices. One might give many reasons for this, but as for me, I saw in it the hand of God.

Then look: Parachuted in from Japan, I found myself elected to be General! I can assure you that at this macroscopic level, one thinks a lot, asks advice, informs oneself, and so on. Even so, things turn out differently and turn out better. We live in a state of trust which does not result in inaction. As St. Ignatius says, we ought to do all that we can, but in the end what counts is trust in God.

Thus in all things, from the time when I used to visit the prisons of New York and meet with hardened criminals, to today when I must decide on the action of the Society when it is faced with the problems, for example, of refugees and the drug culture, I see in these tragic situations not only how weak man is, but also how the Lord intervenes to save him.

Chapter 14

THE ORDINARY GOVERNING OF THE SOCIETY

JEAN-CLAUDE DIETSCH——*How does the Superior General of more than 26,000 Jesuits, who are working in more than a hundred countries, go about his daily work?*

PEDRO ARRUPE——First of all, we must remember that the General has four immediate collaborators, four Assistants and General Counselors who are elected, like him, by the General Congregation, two other General Counselors, and a dozen Regional Assistants whom he himself names after he has consulted his General Assistants and the Provincials of the corresponding regions. Thus, I have around me a team whose members are acquainted with the Society in an especially competent way. They know its structures, its apostolates, and the countries in which the Jesuits are carrying out these apostolates. At present the members of this team belong to thirteen different nationalities.

I ought to mention here, also, the fifteen offices and secretariats whose directors fulfill for me, and therefore for the Society, a function of experts and executive relays.

—— *People say that the government of the Society is very centralized.*

—— It is centralized, that is true; but it is not an autocracy, and still less is it a kind of dictatorship. Yes, according to St. Ignatius, the General has complete authority "for building up" the Society (*ad aedificationem,* in *Constitutions,* [736]). He ought to interpret and carry out God's will for the Society; that is, he ought to use all the means possible for knowing this will. Therefore we see how essential it is for him to gather information and use consultation.

In regard to the written information, which is addressed to me directly, we receive each year here at our General Curia in Rome, some 17,000 letters, among which are the official reports that we call "letters of office" or obligation (*lettres de charge*). They are sent in annually, in about February or March, by all the superiors throughout the Society, and also by their consultors and directors of works. Each one writes according to his own point of view, his own opinions, and his own temperament. Thus, since each situation is described by at least four persons, I receive a balanced and objective perception of the situations.

Of course, I cannot read all these letters in their totality. But, presented and summarized by the Assistants and their secretaries, they all pass through my hands. At times someone says: "It all gets screened out." But that is unthinkable—I have complete confidence in my co-workers. Besides, it is impossible—all the letters reach me, along with their summaries.

As for the consultations, they occur, first of all, in the form of frequent meetings, either regularly scheduled or informal, and long or brief, with the General Assistants and Consultants, with the Regional Assistants, and with those responsible for the secretariats and offices. That brings about an amazing exchange of information, advice, and opinions. But you yourself are a witness of this since, as director of the Society's "Press and Information Office," you attend everything. You are the one, Father Dietsch, who should be giving this point of information.

—— *Even within the Society, some often look on my work with a certain wonderment.*

—— I would not have created a Press and Information Office while refusing to its director the means of knowing what happens day by day in the Society. It is up to you to have the required boldness and prudence to make known the activities of our Order while having regard for the men in it. On the other hand, your function is not that of an "official spokesman," even if some call you that; but you are an observer, or better yet, a witness who, in his own way, informs the Society about itself and the outside world about the Society. Each director of this Office has had his "style"; you have yours. I can inform you of my agreement or disagreement on what you publish, or reproach you for being too talkative on certain points—with you that has rarely been the case!—or of being too brief about other points. I know that you are often begged for information, importunately; but formed in the school of the Spiritual Exercises, you have to choose what is suitable or not. Your task is not easy, and I personally know its hidden reefs. Just think of the sensational headlines which announced that the Jesuits would return to China! They stemmed from a few remarks dropped during a press conference at Rome in March, 1979. Well, so be it! We take our risks.

—— *Let us get back to your work at the Curia.*

—— In addition to the meetings of which we have spoken, I personally meet once a week, under ordinary circumstances, with each one of the Regional Assistants.

However, I wish especially to insist on the following point: The most characteristic form of the government of the Society, and the form most specific to it, is found in what is called the "manifestation of conscience."[1]

—— *There is often questioning about this when Jesuits are spoken of by those outside the Society, and even more so when they are being caricatured. Therefore, it is necessary to state precisely the framework in which it is given.*

—— The manifestation of conscience given to Superiors and to Father General makes it possible for us to know a person well—a person for whom we are responsible with regard to his apostolic work. For the Society and for the success of the missions which are to be carried out, it is so essential that the Society is the only religious institute which is able to impose it juridically. Of course, it is preferable that the manifestation of conscience be given freely and

1 [Manifestation of "conscience" was prescribed by St. Ignatius in his *Constitutions,* (91). As he describes it, there and elsewhere, it was the candid opening up of one's attitude or consciousness or outlook in order that decisions, guidance, or assignments might be reached with understanding and satisfaction better for both superior and subject. Editor.]

without any obligation. But when the obligation of manifestation of conscience was suppressed for all religious congregations, Pope Pius XI granted to Father Ledochowski, then the General, that it be maintained in the Society of Jesus. For, through our vocation, and for the greater good of the Church and of the Society, we ought to have the greatest efficiency possible in our government.

This specific relation to the members makes the government of the Society very original. When we invited here to the Curia the best experts of the MBO (Management by Objectives) to advise us, they all had similar reactions: "We have nothing to teach you; St. Ignatius has already said it all in your *Constitutions*." Also, "we bring you some techniques of administration, of classification, and the like; but that is all. You have a government totally different from others." And why is that? Because we are not in the business world whose criterion is exterior efficiency and profit. We work with the whole person, and what is interior (his character, his difficulties) counts enormously.

Another determining factor is this. We must be able to count on the goodwill of each and every one of our members. In other administrations, the officials continually check the account books, the punctuality, and the like. But we have more confidence in what the person himself tells us than in all the other things. This antecedent confidence in the individual member is not only the foundation of our government but is also, and in very fact, the most dynamic force in our government. For a man who feels himself to be trusted develops all his potentialities, whereas he would be inhibited and blocked if someone showed him reticence or suspicion.

—— *It is not only with the members of the Curia that you have personal contact. It is the same with the Provincials, isn't it?*

—— Oh, yes! We have instituted formation sessions for Provincials, especially those who have just been named. They meet here and live together for two weeks. There are no lectures, but they exchange among themselves their experience, their misgivings, and their hopes. They are the ones who do the speaking, not experts or technicians even if that is useful at times. I am with them all the time and have long conversations with each one. Thus, I know them personally very well, and they know one another.

—— *To how many Jesuit names can you attach a face?*

—— Not to the names of all Jesuits! But, to give an example, of the two hundred thirty-six members of the 32nd General Congregation, which assembled in 1974-75, I personally knew—and interiorly, if one may say that—more than two hundred of them. Thus, for the Superior General, that group did not resemble in any way a political assembly or a parliament. It is something entirely different.

—— *As regards this personal acquaintance with the Jesuits, it is also necessary to note your penchant for travel. You like to meet your men in the actual place of their apostolic work.*

—— I do not do that uniquely in function of what you call my "penchant for travel" but also because the 31st and 32nd General Congregation recommended these journeys. My two predecessors, Fathers Ledochowski and Janssens, traveled only very little. As for me, I have the possibility to do so, and that is not without a decisive influence upon my style of governing. I recall faces, I have met the people, I have visited the works. Practically, I have visited all the provinces and almost all the important works of the Society. Afterwards, of course, the memory plays its part!

There is a complementary aspect too, for I am not the only one to travel. Many people come to Rome. I have met many of them, if only at my table for a meal, and that enables me to know them, to listen directly to the information they bring, and to have long conversations with them, including a few jokes.

—— *I have not been in the Society so very long. But according to what I hear said and what I note myself, this is a rather new situation, isn't it?*

—— I can only agree. Just consider the time that was necessary in the past to come from Japan to Rome or to go from Rome to Australia: weeks and weeks. There is also the telephone, which has provided a tremendous facility for government. If a letter is not clear, I can call its writer; "Is this what you wanted to say?"—"Oh no, not at all!'' It is a bit because of that that I say we are able to be more Ignatian than St. Ignatius.

—— It is true that there has been technical progress in communications. But Jesuits, whatever the means of locomotion, have always traveled a great deal; the fathers who work in the archives have pointed out to me several times biographies which indicate extraordinary mobility! My question therefore is more precise. Has there not been, at the Jesuit Curia itself, a change in the psychological atmosphere?

—— Yes, indeed, there has been. The Curia was considered somewhat of a "taboo" place. There were fathers who entered this house of the Curia only after they had lived in Rome thirty years! Still today a few fathers say, "I didn't think the Curia was like this." I answer facetiously, "We aren't cannibals here, you know!" We try to be, in spite of our size—there are a good hundred of us—a simple, welcoming, brotherly community.

The introduction, in the refectory, of small tables for five people in place of the long tables against the walls constituted a sort of revolution. That—and many other things (like the creation of a "bar" with fruit juices and cola drinks—what a fuss there was about choosing the brand!) contributed to contacts which are more personal, to a deeper level of communication.

—— All this ease of having meetings that results from the travels of Jesuits to and fro and face-to-face contacts, does it not make the government too personalized?

—— Personalized, perhaps; too personalized, I think not. Take for example the nomination of provincials, who are the key men for the government of the Society. The process has developed a great deal. We make preliminary soundings, we study what the necessary qualities are according to conditions lived out in the province. Thus, as successor to a very active man, perhaps a calmer person is necessary; after a man most interested in schools, perhaps a man more oriented toward pastoral work is required; after an administrator, perhaps a more charismatic man. But, in the end, there is no vote; it is I who must make the choice in view of all the information received and after having heard the advice of my counselors. Besides, it is important that I know very personally the Jesuits whose names are proposed to me.

—— *Sometimes an "Arrupe era" is spoken of. What do you think of that?*

—— Bah! It is evident that I am different from each of my predecessors. But it is necessary to be aware of one thing; Jesuits hate the cult of personality. One sign is this. You have often noticed that, at mealtime during assembly in the dining room, the place taken last is the one next to the General—that is, of course, when no guest is present.

No, we do not function with respect to persons—except on a few great occasions of affective manifestations, with applause and the like. I remember the first time that I took a trip, almost all the community was at the door to greet me; and it was very embarrassing! Now it is much more simple, happily!

Truly, I believe it is very Jesuit-like to practice the demythologizing of personality.

—— *However, don't you need the expression of marks of approbation or encouragement?*

—— If it is a matter of saying to me, "Oh, Father, I really like you!"—no, I don't need that. But to see that the men understand my ideas and follow my directives, for me that is encouragement. To observe that a letter has been accepted and has done some good is also a consolation.

I think relations ought to be virile, not affective, not emotional, and especially not diplomatic. Diplomacy destroys authority and would be a poison for the government of the Society. It may happen that a pastoral approach which is inspired by charity resembles diplomacy, from the outside and for a period of time; but in reality it is never diplomacy. If a Jesuit has the impression that his superior is a diplomat, true relations are ended. And also if the superior lacks discretion, even indirectly and without quoting anyone, about the content of the manifestation of conscience, the relations are ended. The secrecy of the manifestation of conscience is sacred.

Chapter 15

_____

THE "FOURTH VOW"

JEAN-CLAUDE DIETSCH——*Before I ask you questions about the relations between the Society of Jesus and the Holy See, and more specifically, between the Superior General and the Sovereign Pontiff, you would like your readers to reread an extract from one of your conferences. Given on February 18, 1978, it had as a title*[1] "To Serve the Lord Alone and the Church, His Spouse, under the Roman Pontiff, the Vicar of Christ on Earth."[2]

PEDRO ARRUPE——The substance of what I stated is this:

"The vow of obedience to the pope is the 'principal foundation'[3] of the Society for a reason otherwise important and profound than the circumstantial facts which condition its structure; it is a question of the orientation which it gives to the Society. Apart from the obligation, in the strict sense, which flows from the vow, there is no doubt that the vow breathes into the whole body of the Society a spirit of special devotion and fidelity to the Holy See, which other religious institutes do not necessarily have. This is the reason why Pope Paul VI, confirming the thought of his predecessors, mentioned among the four characteristics of the Society that of being 'united to the Roman Pontiff by a special bond of love and service.' In reality, the Society has always lived this spirit 'of love and service' to the Sovereign Pontiff, as history demonstrates. Friends

_____

1 [The conference is in P. Arrupe, *Challenge to Religious Life Today,* pp. 253-277. See pp. 259-262 for the extract in question. Editor.]

2 [*Exposcit debitum,* 3,1). This is the papal Formula of the Institute of the Society of Jesus, dated July 21, 1550. Editor.]

3 [". . . quasi totius Societatis fundamentum," a phrase of Bl. Pierre Favre's

and enemies have unanimously recognized it, either to defend the Society or to condemn it.''

—— *This has given the general orientation. But how is it expressed in the daily life of the Jesuits?*

—— The vow of obedience to the Sovereign Pontiff—our fourth vow—and the spirit of this vow constitute for St. Ignatius the origin and foundation of the Society of Jesus. This is why this vow and its spirit pervade all our *Constitutions* as well as our spirituality. This vow, therefore, ought to be carefully interpreted. We should be aware of the obligations that it implies and the spirit it engenders. There are some persons who think that, from a strictly juridical point of view, it concerns only ''the sending on a mission''; others think that it has a wider import. I, for my part, think that it has a wider import. The Holy Father is the highest Superior of the Society, and all the doctrine of obedience established by St. Ignatius ought to be applied to him. And that should be done with the greatest sincerity. The Holy Father represents Jesus Christ; we ought to love him, we ought to defend him, and we ought to study and explain his doctrine.

That certainly does not prevent us from having also, according to St. Ignatius, the duty of ''representation'' with all its conditions.[4] For example, the ''representation'' is not necessarily public, especially with the mass media, which tend to transform all ''representation'' into a spectacle or an opposition. Our obedience is not passive; we have the availability of free persons. But it is true that, as Jesuits, once all the representations are made, we practice evangelical obedience; it is Jesus Christ who by his vicar and the superiors of the Society sends us. This is the basic apostolic dimension. Everything comes in here: Trinitarian love, fidelity to Christ, love of the Church, discernment, availability, mobility, loyalty; such is the Ignatian concept.

It is sometimes said, in the Society itself, that in what concerns obedience the power also comes from the community. This

Memoriale, no. 18, found also in *Fontes narrativi de S Ignacio,* I, 42. Editor.]

4 [On representation, see *Constitutions of the Society of Jesus,* (543, 610, 627); also, Ignatius' letter of March 26, 1553, on Obedience, no. 19. Editor.]

democractic concept is not Ignatian. The community may intervene as an element of discernment for the superiror, but the true power follows a vertical path.

—— *Concretely, what are the relations with the Holy Father?*

—— We do not constitute another "Swiss Guard" of the Holy Father. No, no! But we do owe full loyalty to the Holy Father.

We have a special spirit of fidelity toward the Sovereign Pontiff. Naturally, the first one who ought to have this spirit is myself. Even more than all the other Jesuits, as General I must listen, understand, and carry out his desires and his will. It is not a question of "politics," but of service. I am also able, as St. Ignatius himself did, to express to the Holy Father our concept of religious life, what we are and what we do. Again, it is a question of serving.

—— *We cannot fail to note that, upon this basis of essential collaboration, the history of the Society is also marked by tensions with the Sovereign Pontiffs and the members of the hierarchy.*

—— These tensions are in the very nature of things. They bring into relief what the Society is and does, from its direct experience of the apostolate, from its avant-garde position, from its involvement in controverted questions—and also at times from personalities. By vocation, a Jesuit whose apostolate is exercised directly can risk more than a member of the hierarchy, or more than a Nuncio, who must be aware of the whole ecclesial ensemble. Thus, it is normal that some tensions are produced between the hierarchical and the charismatic dimension, between the administrative and prophetic dimensions. Assuredly, all these dimensions should in the end be integrated; but such an integration is not immediately and easily brought about. It is necessary to recall that if the Church is the Spouse of Christ, it is also incarnated. We are men, and people say, is it not a great miracle that, in spite of our weaknesses and errors, the Church continues?

But there is something more important than these tensions, real as they are at every step in the Society's life. One must live obedience; and especially for a Jesuit formed in the school of the *Spiritual Exercises* and therefore disposed to follow Christ totally, obedience is a mystery which includes the Cross; but the Cross itself is an act of obedience to the Father so that life may be communicated to us and that we may in our turn communicate it. If our faith in the dead and risen Christ is weakened—and that has happened at times to Jesuits—then our obedience is impoverished and discussions, criticisms, demands, and the like begin.

—— *Your generalate has taken place during the pontificates of Paul VI, John Paul I, and John Paul II. Could you speak of their relations with the Society and yourself?*

—— To explain these relations I shall speak especially of Paul VI. In fact, of the Sovereign Pontiffs I have known as Superior General, it is Paul VI whom I knew for the longest time and with whom I was most intimately associated.

The bonds between Paul VI and the Society go back to his childhood, and he has often spoken with evident affection of the Jesuits he had known when he was beginning his studies. He always showed a high esteem for the Society and kept great confidence in it, even when he was sharing with us and clearly expressing his fear that he was seeing the Society hesitating or falling into error in its mission.

His great concern was that the Society should remain faithful; and it is true that we have given him, at different moments, some reasons for anxiety. His solicitude and even at times his anxiety were not only personal—due to his long association with the Jesuits—but also ecclesial. He repeated to me several times: The influence of the Society is enormous, and its experience is not without important consequences for the whole of religious life and for the entire Church. I used to find myself facing a father who wants his son to behave well. After the audiences, I felt encouraged, even if I took a lot of chiding! Our relations were very cordial.

—— *This is not, nevertheless, the image that has sometimes been given!*

—— That is because the media of social communication, the press among others, generally report only the negative things and pass over the positive. This was the case long ago, and still is the case today. Without doubt it belongs to the nature of the mass media to "dramatize"; but before an ensemble of systematic distortions, I wonder if there is not, in the background, a campaign against one or another institution.

Thus, year after year Paul VI was given an image which was without balance; they did not stop repeating that he was sad, agonized, and what not else. But this was not true!

Likewise, look how his speeches to our last General Congregation were quoted; and nevertheless, he had also said many very beautiful things about the Society. Indeed, he had pointed out the dangers we were running, but all the other things? They were passed over in silence!

—— *Even so, there were some tensions at the time of the 32nd General Congregation. Did not Paul VI strongly intervene?*

—— The Holy Father intervened only because we had not then understood certain points that he wanted us to take into consideration, particularly in what concerns the "grades" in the Society (professed with four vows, spiritual coadjutors, temporal coadjutors). We had believed—and even voted—that this was an open question about which the members of the Congregation were able to exchange their opinions. But for the Holy Father, this was a fundamental point of our Institute and could not in any way be changed. When, following an audience with the Sovereign Pontiff, I made his decisive opinion known to the fathers in the Congregation, all accepted it without discussion. That was for me one of the best examples of total obedience in the Society, and I have a great admiration for this Congregation.

And it is certain that the Society has been aided by the insistence of this reminder: Whatever may be the choices we make for our ministries, they should be accomplished in conformity with the fundamental principles of our Order, just as those principles were conceived in the beginning by St. Ignatius and specified in our Institute.

It was also because Paul VI felt highly responsible for the Society that he, through the intermediary of Cardinal Villot (letter of May

2, 1975), called our attention to the delicate aspects of certain decrees which had been voted. We have indeed seen these aspects turn up in the application of these decrees, and we are well aware of them today: risks of confusion between the promotion of justice and political engagement, risks of forgetting the spiritual dimension of our ministries and in this way impoverishing the life of prayer; or risks of forgetfulness of the Ignatían charism, or a tendency toward a disincarnated spirituality, and so on.

In these remarks of the Holy Father there was not any abusive interference or excessive display of authority, but fatherly solicitude. Their acceptance by the whole Society remains, for me, a criterion of its health.

—— *How does the Holy Father know about the Society of Jesus on a day-to-day basis? Has he other sources of information than the Father General?*

—— Of course! He is able to have numerous contacts with the Jesuits who work as experts at the Vatican and with those who belong to the different congregations and secretariats. There are also all the personal visits and audiences. From their side, the bishops inform the pope on the work of the Society in their respective regions. Remember also that Paul VI was personally interested in the reviews published by the Jesuits.

—— *It has been said that the image of the Society has suffered somewhat from the fact that certain Jesuits had not accepted either the 31st or the 32nd General Congregation. What did these Jesuit represent?*

—— Numerically, out of the whole Society, they were not at all numerous, and they are even less so today. They had attached an absolute value to the remarks and the reservations of the Holy Father. In addition, they held restrictive views on the meaning of the priestly ministry of the Society; they found ambiguous the theological research which is developing, just as one of their main difficulties resided in the evolution of the liturgy.

Besides, certain ones among them, like some other religious in different orders, were depending on the hope of being able to constitute independent groups, with autonomous novitiates, and the like. They caused the Society to undergo a very grave danger. In great part it was to confirm the orientations of the 31st General Congregation and to reinforce the unity of the Society that the 32nd General Congregation was convoked in 1974-1975.

—— *Did these Jesuits, in some way, wish to set the Society directed by Father Arrupe in opposition to the one founded by St. Ignatius?*

—— I certainly hope that that is not possible, either yesterday or today! In reality, what is my fundamental task, with the collaboration of my assistants and counselors? To understand, as profoundly as possible, the Ignatian charism in order to give it the most extensive application possible in our time.

Throughout history, you have the different realizations of the Ignatian charism. We must go back to what is not incarnated, that is to say, the spirit of the founder. We cannot opt for one or the other of its realizations and, by doing so, limit a priori the applications of the first charism.

I must first of all follow Ignatius the Founder, and only afterwards Ignatius the General. For there are dimensions of the Ignatian charism which we understand better now, given the global development of societies. For example, community life, insertion into the world, discernment, poverty, and even obedience; or also universality, which St. Ignatius felt more than understood. It is in this perspective that I say, once again, that we are able to be more Ignatian than St. Ignatius.

Thus it is clear that today the true Jesuit community is the entire body of the Society, and not a house which some in the past conceived somewhat like a "fortress." The Jesuit went out from it in order to accomplish his task and then returned to the shelter of its "ramparts" to regain his strength. We are from now on integrated into the world like the yeast in the dough, and we may find ourselves working alone without the framework of a particular community.

It is also clear that this enlarged apostolic dimension implies a deeper spirituality than ever and a more intense life of prayer.

Universal availability and robust spirituality: These ought to be the characteristic traits of the Society today, in fidelity to the Ignatian charism. I recalled this at the congregation of procurators in September 1978. But I did it with nuances, because the orientations of the 31st and 32nd General Congregations, which applied the spirit of Vatican II to the life of the Jesuits, are still on the way to realization and are not yet equally assimilated by all. Evidently, the response to questions so profound and complex as these, which are at the same time spiritual and human, requires time.

—— At this congregation of procurators, it was very apparent that all the provinces were working at the application of the decrees voted in 1965-1966 and in 1974-1975. This application was following different rhythms, perhaps slower rather than faster. Don't you think you went too fast in announcing, in 1980, that you would propose—as one of those decrees[5] authorized—your resignation at a future general congregation?

—— I answer you clearly: No. After personal discernment and with the opinion of my General Assistants, I believe that I made this decision at an opportune moment. Before God, I felt that this decree applied to my situation.

I am the interpreter and executor of the decrees voted by the General Congregation composed of elected members. The elected representatives (the General Assistants) whom the Congregation placed at my side, and who, among numerous tasks, have the one of watching over the Father General, had given their agreement to my interpretation of the decree on resignation.

As for the precise date, it had been determined in relation to another element of the Society's legislation: the convocation of the Congregation of Provincials, three years after that of the Congregation of Procurators.

—— In your applying, yourself, the decree which authorizes a Father General to offer his resignation under certain conditions, were you not wanting also to reinforce the value of the other decrees, by giving a rather spectacular example?

5 [Decree 41 of the 31st General Congregation. Editor.]

—— Not at all. This argument never entered into my considerations. But I did think that this decree was to be applied, first of all, to show detachment from power and authority. Then there was another reason: to make this decree function in the purest, clearest way. This decree is good and applicable, and there is no reason to come back later to the question of election for life. Election of the general for life remains; it is a basic Ignatian intuition, and I was one of the most fervent defenders of it. However, the General Congregation made a prudential decree. I show that this decree is good and, for me, opportune.

★ ★ ★

During the weeks which followed these interviews, I transcribed the tapes. Father Arrupe completed a first reading of the text and wrote a few pages of conclusion for me. We set aside some time during the month of August to do a second reading together and to make some additions on either a period of time or a theme.

What then happened is well known. Stricken with a cerebral thrombosis on August 7, 1981, Father Arrupe spent a month in the hospital. Since then he has been in the infirmary of the General Curia, where [as of late 1981] his condition continues to improve weekly. He always receives me with his same warm, smiling welcome, but it is impossible for him to take up again the dialogue which was so cruelly interrupted. It was not even possible for him to reread the text which I had clarified according to some of his comments.

Thus, the text of his conclusion, written in June of 1981, takes on a very special value.

Chapter 16

CONCLUSION

As co-author now turned reader, I have just reviewed these pages. Do I recognize myself in them? Partially, yes. If I did not recognize myself in their sum total, it is not the fault of Father Dietsch, who has done a magnificent job, but my own fault. For it is impossible to express everything. In the life of each person there is an intimate dimension that cannot be communicated.

Biographies are always unfinished portraits. In many matters, the light that is hidden within the depths of our being is lacking. If that light could be brought out, it would transform our image radically. But it cannot be imparted; its only value is in remaining hidden.

True biography is written only before the Lord. He alone is the one who can correct and add many things, sometimes those most precious elements which go unnoticed even by ourselves. Before the Lord—that is to say, as St. John of the Cross described it, "In the blessed night / hidden from others / and looking at nothing / without other guide or light / than that which burns in the heart."

Someone has written, I don't know where, that the most interesting biography is that which is written "without ink." That remark can, doubtless, be applied to the preceding pages. It calls to mind especially the words of St. Paul to the Corinthians, "You are a letter from Christ,. . . written not with ink, but with the Spirit of the living God" (2 Cor. 3:3).

I have the impression that my life is written in a single sentence; "It has unfolded according to the will of God." It is summed up in the *fiat voluntas tua*—"Thy will be done" (Matt. 26:42). That can be said and written easily, but I myself do not understand either concretely or fully what it means. It is the mystery of all human life, which will only be revealed on the day when we see ourselves reflected in the face of God, when we shall find ourselves "face to face" with him (1 Cor. 13:12).

This does not mean that I consider my life to be especially extraordinary. The extraordinary thing is that, although I have been much lacking in what the orientation of my life should have been, the Lord continued to make possible his plan in my life. He loves us as we are, and He has loved me as I am. The miracle of life resides in this love which disposes, helps, and sustains. Marvelous things occur in everyone's life, and it is this same love of God which makes them appear as if they were our own doing, whereas in reality they are his work. One finds here all over again the great difficulty in marking the border between the human and the divine.

In retracing all the steps of my life with their concrete details and exterior manifestations, I arrive at the same conclusion: That which is most important and most decisive in my life, that which characterizes it as most personal, cannot be communicated—either because it is a question of intimate experiences which cannot be translated into words, or because these experiences themselves have a value that is very personal and interior—and it is because something remains hidden that it is, precisely, a value.

As I read these pages, I wondered if we should not start over. But no, we would come up against the same obstacle and never achieve satisfaction. I resign myself to appear, on the one hand, better than I really am, since my most intimate limitations are not described, and on the other hand, less than I really am, since the most intimate part of my life remains unexpressed and unexplained. And furthermore, since it is a gift of God, it does not belong to me.

The entire book has been about the past. Thus it seems to me that this conclusion should have been written later, when the final years of my life would have slipped away—years which will inevitably pass. But at the end I will perhaps be no longer able to dictate my thoughts. How many years will there be, and how will they unfold? That is yet one more mystery in life. But it is certain that the end will come "when one is least expecting it, . . . like a thief" (Luke 12:39-40).

In reality, death, which is sometimes feared so much, is for me one of the most anticipated events, an event that will give meaning to my life. Death can be considered as the end of life or as the threshold of eternity; in both of these aspects I find consolation. In the first instance, as the end of life, it is still the end of a life which is nothing else than a path crossing the desert to approach eternity—sometimes a very difficult path, on which, as one's physical strength diminishes, the burden of the years becomes heavier. Inasmuch as death is also the threshold of eternity, it involves the entrance into an eternity which is at the same time unknown and yet longed for; it involves meeting the Lord and an eternal intimacy with him. Like St. Paul, I feel myself "torn in two ways; I desire to depart and be with Christ" (Phil. 1:23), but "I do not refuse to work," if I can be useful, so long as the Lord wills it.

Eternity, immortality, beatific vision, perfect happiness—it is all new, nothing is known. Is death a leap into a void? No, of course not. It is to throw yourself into the arms of the Lord; it is to hear the invitation, unmerited, but given in all sincerity, "Well done, good and faithful servant; . . . come and enter into the joy of your master" (Matt. 25:21); it is to come to the end of faith and hope in order to live in eternal and infinite love (1 Cor. 13:8). What will heaven be like? It is impossible to imagine. It is "that which eye has not seen, nor ear heard, nor has it entered into the heart of man what God has prepared for those who love Him" (1 Cor. 2:9). I hope that it will be a *consummatum est*—"all is finished," the final *Amen* of my life and the first *Alleluia* of my eternity.

Fiat, fiat.

Pedro Arrupe, S.J.
June, 1981.

Chapter 17

ROOTED AND GROUNDED IN LOVE
(Ephesians 3:17)

Editor's Introduction

In the late 1970's the Ignatian Center of Spirituality, located in the Jesuit Curia in Rome, offered annually a five-week course of lectures on one or another aspect of Jesuit spirituality. The lectures were given by well-known speakers or authors, drawn from the Society's curial staff, Jesuit Historical Institute, or one of the Jesuit universities in Rome. The audience, often numbering well over 100, consisted of Jesuits, religious women and men, and lay persons.

In 1979, 1980, and 1981 Father Arrupe gave, as the concluding lecture of the respective courses, a trilogy of addresses on "the inspirational sources of the Ignatian charism." His topics were: "Our Manner of Proceeding," on January 19, 1979; "The Trinitarian Inspiration of the Ignatian Charism," on February 8, 1980; and "Rooted and Grounded in Love," February 6, 1981.

Father Arrupe—a rapid, dynamic, and enthusiastic speaker—manifestly put his whole heart into his last address, which in turn manifests his own personality and interior life. He was aiming, as he told his hearers, "to penetrate to the very core of this supreme Ignatian experience: the reality that 'God is love'" (1 John 4:8). His sections no. 4-12 form a miniature commentary on St. Ignatius' Spiritual Exercises, and nos. 13-15 are a similar commentary on the spirit of Ignatius' Constitutions of the Society of Jesus.

His concluding section (nos. 75-83) on the the Heart of Jesus as the résumé and symbol of love, was pronounced by him, as many

105

of his hearers reported, with a special sincerity and emphasis which made them listen in silence and attentive awe. To no small extent this section turned out to be a sort of will or spiritual legacy. For later, on August 7 of that same year 1981, he suffered the stroke which left him largely incapacitated.

An outline of his talk follows.

Chapter 18

"ROOTED AND GROUNDED IN LOVE"
(Ephesians 3:17)

Introduction: A trilogy of addresses on the inspirational sources of the Ignatian charism

1. This is the third time that I have accepted the invitation of the Center of Ignatian Spirituality to give the closing address at the annual Ignatian Course. In 1979 I dealt with "Our Way of Proceeding" ("Nuestro Modo de Proceder"), and last year I spoke on "The Trinitarian Inspiration of the Ignatian Charism." In both cases I sought to contribute to the study of the inspirational sources of our charism: This is the path that the Second Vatican Council indicates to Religious Institutes to work at their updating renewal ("accommodata renovatio"[1]). The first address on "Our Way of Proceeding" took its starting point from the Ignatian charism and *worked its way down* through various levels of application to the changed conditions of the times,[2] whereas the second on "The Trinitarian Inspiration," while also starting from the charism of Ignatius, *moved upwards* even to its peak-point: its Trinitarian intimacy. Today I propose to penetrate to *the very core* of this

1 These three addresses were first published as nos. 42, 45, and 47 of the series "Documentation" which is published in Rome by the Press and Information Office of the Society of Jesus. Father Arrupe later republished them as Letters to the Whole Society in the official *Acta Romana Societatis Iesu,* where they are printed in the original Spanish and in English and French translations. They are found respectively in Volumes XVII, fasciculus iii (1979), 653-757; XVIII, i (1980), 66-215; and XVIII, ii (1981), 431-538, with the English on 472-504. This English version is reproduced here.
2 In Vatican Council II, decree on the Updated Renewal of Religious Life, no. 2.

supreme Ignatian experience: the reality that "God is love."[3] For, in my opinion, this is the final summing-up and synthesis of all that Ignatius learned in that privileged Trinitarian intimacy to which he was graciously called: *The divine unity between the Father and the Son culminates, as a society of love, in the relationship that both have with the one Spirit.*[4] This is, therefore, the very last root, the ultimate foundation of the Ignatian charism, the soul of the Society.

2. As far as one can deal with these matters in human terms, one could say that love at its purest—love in itself—is, on the one hand, the formal constitutive element of the divine essence and, on the other, the explanation and cause of the operations outward, 'ad extra': the creation of man, lord of the universe, and the return of all things to God in a history of redemption and sanctification. This double formal aspect of love finds in Ignatius the echo of a double response: a sublime theocentric love that is compatible with a marked presence of Christ even as man; and a boundless love of charity for his fellow men in whom God's love, as he sees it, is patently present, and who must be led back to God. If then we want this updated renewal (*renovatio accommodata*) to work itself out in us with the Ignatian depth of the *Exercises,* which start from the deepest level of man's heart, we shall have to let ourselves be invaded by that love that is the peak-point of the Ignatian charism. Created as we are in the image and likeness of God who is love, we shall thus become more like Him. This love will be the force (*dynamis*) of our apostolic character; this love it is that will enable us to collaborate in the solution of the tremendous problems so characteristic of our world which is in the throes of radical change to a new age.

3. Any renewal that does not somehow reach up to this point, any renewal that leaves the heart of man untouched and unpurified, is a renewal that is incomplete and doomed to failure. If, however, our inmost faculties are purified and transformed, we shall have been given a completely new orientation: The renewal

3 1 John 4:8
4 The Trinitarian Inspiration of the Ignatism Charism, no. 99, in *ActRSJ,* XVIII, i (1980), 157-158.

will not give rise to traumas, we shall be placed on a higher plane on which the various dichotomies and tensions fade away—between faith and justice, for instance, when both are vivified by love—and we shall act out of mercy that is the sublimation of justice. With this spirit, "rooted and grounded in love," the Society will continue to be the shock-troops in the confrontation between wickedness and love—between *anomía* and *agápe,* to use the terms in which St. Matthew couches the Lord's apocalyptic discourse, terms so terribly applicable to our age.[5]

I. LOVE AND CHARITY IN THE SOCIETY OF JESUS

4. "Love is the weighty power of the soul."[6] This is what Ignatius wrote to a former companion and fellow-student of his Paris days, without knowing perhaps that he was quoting St. Augustine. And certainly, without intending to do so, he was bequeathing to us the most incisive formulation possible of his own spiritual journey, and of the charism of the Society.

1. In the Exercises

When Ignatius concludes the *Exercises,* his "to praise, reverence, and serve God" of the Principle and Foundation[7] has become a "Contemplation to Attain Love."[8] A love which "ought to manifest itself in deeds rather than in words"[8] and in "giving and sharing."[9] These two qualities of the love of the exercitant, who has put order into his life, correspond to identical qualities that Ignatius has contemplated in the love of God: God not only "so loved the world that He gave us His only Son,"[10] but—and we must "ponder this with great affection"—"He desires to give Himself to me, as far as He can, according to His divine decrees."[11] This love

5 Matt. 24:12.
6 Letter to Manuel Sanches, Bishop of Targa, from Rome, May 18, 1547, in *EppIgn.* I, 513-515.
7 *SpEx,* [23].
8 Ibid., [230].
9 Ibid., [231].
10 John 3:16.
11 *SpEx,* [234].

is to lead the exercitant to the point where, "filled with gratitude," that is, in a return of love for love, he "may in all things love and serve the Divine Majesty." [12] To serve is to give oneself.

5. This conclusion is not surprising. The role of the director is to lead the exercitant to discover this love. His mission is "not to urge the exercitant more to poverty... than to the contrary ...but... it is much better that the Creator and Lord in person communicate Himself to the devout soul, that He inflame it with His love and praise, and dispose it for the way in which it could better serve God in the future."[13] Once again there appears the relationship between love and service, for with Ignatius service, or the gift of oneself, is a necessary expression of love. In other words: One cannot love without serving. Service is love in return for love, it is the way in which one gives oneself. The exercitant is to consider, "according to all reason and justice, what I ought to offer the Divine Majesty, that is, all I possess and myself with it."[14] To attain this love is the highest grace one seeks: "Take and receive... Thou hast given all to me. To Thee I return it... Give me Thy love and Thy grace, for this is sufficient for me."

6. It is interesting to note that the pedagogy of love in the *Exercises* seems to follow the exact lines of the pedagogy of love in Old Testament revelation. It is not a theory of love that is propounded, but an experiential pedagogy that is practiced. Love is presented as the constant agent of all that leads to salvation: from creation—"the other things...are created for man"—to the barricade set up between man and hell, even unto the plan of redemption, the call to reciprocal love and to the service of cooperation. One might say that Ignatius puts his exercitant under a sort of irresistible pressure of proofs of the love of God, a love that is made manifest more in deeds than in words through repeated acts of self-giving that culminate in the surrender and gift of His only Son. In this way Ignatius means to set in motion a process of complete transformation in the exercitant: the purification of his heart and the right

12 *SpEx,* [233].
13 *SpEx,* [15].
14 *SpEx,* [234].

ordering of his affective faculty. In a word, his objective is to get the exercitant to live the truth of God's own love and his love for God by giving himself in service.

7. From the *First Week* on, love is a definite criterion. Consolation and desolation—which, as we know, are the precision tools in the whole process of change—have precisely the presence or absence of love for their determinant difference (*Rules 3,4,9*).[15] In the Second Week it is love that is the axis of the great decisions. In the first meditation (the Earthly King) there will still be mention of "giving greater proof of love and distinguishing self in whatever concerns service," precisely as a reaction "against carnal and worldly love,"[16] because the whole attractiveness of the love of God has not yet been explicitly proposed. In fact, the preliminary phase of purification has barely been concluded with the First Week. The contemplation of the mysteries of Christ, which then begin almost unexpectedly, are already a strategy of love: the love of God in action, and the response of man who is now capable of lifting on high his gaze of love. "This is to ask for what I desire: an intimate knowledge of the Lord, who has become man for me, that I may love Him more and follow Him more closely."[17] In these exercises, termed very significantly the contemplation of the "mysteries," the pace of the transference of self-love to the love of Christ gains momentum: It is the gift of the love of God. There is an ascent towards perfect love, which keeps moving up by means of the colloquy of the meditation of the Two Standards and of the Three Classes of Men, where there is still *attachment or repugnance*[18] with respect to the consequences of the love of God. It is the surrender *of self-love, self-will and self-interest.*[19]

8. Of deep psychological and theological interest are two important moments in the exercitant's journey in which Ignatius instructs him to reflect on his self-love. The parallelism of both passages shows how clear this idea was in the mind of Ignatius, who had

15 *SpEx,* [316, 317, 322.].
16 *SpEx,* [97].
17 *SpEx,* [104].
18 *SpEx,* [157].
19 *SpEx,* [189].

come close to almost stereotyping his phrases. The two passages deal, one with the 'election' made according to the second way of the third time—a way that is more affective and less cerebral than the first—and the other with the norms for the distribution of ecclesiastical goods. In an effort at introspection and almost cold objective observation of oneself, that is so genuinely Ignatian, the exercitant must make sure that "the love, that moves one and causes one to choose a particular thing, descends from above, that is, from the love of God."[20] It is the guarantee document that the excitant must demand of, and grant to, himself: the identity of love with God. The same precaution is highlighted before one can set about distributing ecclesiastical goods. Of the four things that the exercitant should observe, "the first is that the love that moves me... must be from above, that is, from the love of God our Lord... that God is manifestly the cause of my loving them more"[21]—that is, such persons, be they relatives or friends. What stands out clearly here is the understanding of the close link of causality and reciprocity between the love of God and the love of men.

9. Naturally, one reaches this goal only through a process which originates in one's own ability to love. For, despite the gratuitous accusation made against St. Ignatius with almost mechanical repetition, he by no means ignores nor kills natural love. Ignatius acknowledges and accepts it, indeed he requires it; for only with it, purified and put in order, can one respond to the love of God. Full of meaning is the correction in his own hand and writing in the manuscript of the *Exercises,* one more example of those "second thoughts" of his, so significant for the exact grasp of his mind. The manuscript read in its title: "to order one's life without any attachment that might be inordinate." Ignatius corrected it as follows: "without any decision being made under the influence of any inordinate attachment." In other words, Ignatius knows very well that attachments, even inordinate attachments (that is, attractions inclining one to persons or things because of the love one has for them), will continue to exist. What matters is that one masters the

20 *SpEx,* [184].
21 *SpEx,* [338].

situation in giving the right direction to that love. Ignatius expresses it marvellously in two phrases that have become proverbial: "conquest of self" and "ordering one's life."

10. "To conquer oneself," as Ignatius himself explains, is to "make our sensual nature obey reason,"[22] to master the domain of those attachments and repugnances proper to our fallen nature that obscure the goal of true love. As he says in another part, we have "to overcome the inordinate attachment."[23] This is one of the objectives—the main one—of the stage of purification that culminates in the meditation on hell. It is a logical process in three steps charcterized by three verbs: "to feel (interiorly) the disorder of my actions, that filled with horror of them, I may amend my life and put it in order."[24] Amendment of life is to put order in the disorder of one's actions; it is to prepare the way for love.

11. To order one's life is to apply an ordered love to the great choices in a person's life: It is to let the love of God find the proper response in the life of a man, cutting off all escape-routes or deviations. This is clearly proved by another of Ignatius's manuscript corrections. The text read thus: "Three Classes of Men. Each of them has acquired ten thousand ducats not merely for the love of God."[25] The love of God was not excluded, but it was not exclusive. And this leaves Ignatius dissatisfied, so that he corrects the text: "not purely, or as they should have, for the love of God." The three classes want to rid themselves of the inordinate attachment, but only the third place themselves in the hypothesis "as if every attachment to the sum acquired had been set aside, making efforts neither to want that nor anything else unless the service of God our Lord alone move them to do so." Ignatius lets them know a few lines lower down what they are to do "in order to overcome such an inordinate attachment" or repugnance, as would be with respect to actual poverty: to "act against it" (*agere contra*), begging insistently, "even though corrupt nature rebel against it,"[26] for

22 *SpEx*, [87].
23 *SpEx*, [157].
24 *SpEx*, [63].
25 *SpEx*, [150].
26 *SpEx*, [157].

actual poverty—a point that had already been the key issue of the Two Standards. It is the love of man launched forward to encounter the love of God. The place of encounter is the person of Christ, of whom the exercitant insistently asks for "an interior knowledge of the Lord, that I may love Him more and follow Him more closely."[27] This core group of exercises—the Earthly King, the Two Standards, the Three Classes, the Three Kinds of Humility—purify one's love to the point of a total reversal of values and standards. The exercitant comes to pray for something that is not merely not born of an "inordinate attachment," but even goes beyond just having "judgment and reason: Those who wish to give greater proof of their love, and to distinguish themselves... will act against their sensuality and carnal and worldly love."[28] "The greater service and praise"—indeed, in the last analysis, greater love—can call forth this kind of determined decision from the depths of one who has discovered the love of Christ. And it would seem that greater love than this could not be possible. But St. Ignatius finds it, and invites his exercitant to it, in the Third Kind of Humility, "the most perfect kind." It is the total reversal of 'disorder' and of 'carnal and worldly love,' something that surpasses human logic and shares somehow in that disdain for the purely reasonable which is at the heart of all passionate love. It is no longer necessary that there be "greater service and praise"; it is enough that "whenever the praise and glory of the Divine Majesty be equally served, in order to imitate and be in reality more like Christ our lord, I desire and choose."[29] Are we surprised that so qualified a person as Dr. Ortiz, to whom Ignatius gave the Exercises in Monte Cassino in the Lent of 1548, should write in his notes "Three kinds and degrees of the love of God" in place of the "Three Kinds of Humility"?[30]

12. The *Exercises* are, in the last analysis, a method in the pedagogy of love—the pedagogy, that is, of the most pure charity

27 *SpEx*, [104, 113, 117, 126].
28 *SpEx*, [97, 98].
29 *SpEx*, [167].
30 *Exercitia Spiritualia, Textuum antiquissimorum nova editio*, (1969), Vol. 100 in Monumenta Historica Societatis Iesu, 631, 633.

towards God and towards one's neighbor. They root out of the heart of man carnal and worldly love, thus opening it to the beams of God's love. A demanding love it is, calling forth in man a response of love and of service. Service, which is itself love. This is the message of the very last paragraph of the book of the *Exercises:* "The zealous service of God our Lord out of pure love should be esteemed above all."[31] In the *Exercises* we find terms and concepts which are logically reducible to one another: The 'glory of God', for example, can be replaced by the 'service of God'. The same may be said of 'praise' and 'reverence'. Only one term is final and irreducible to any other: love.

B. *In the* Constitutions

13. Since the Society, when all is said and done, is no more than the institutional expression of the *Exercises,* love that is the keypoint in the *Exercises* must find its parallel in the *Constitutions of the Society of Jesus.* This is so in fact, but with one difference: while the *Exercises* look to conversion and a life-decision on a personal level, the *Constitutions* have a very definite corporate dimension. But the spirit is the same. Moreover, the principal value of the *Constitutions* does not lie in the logical precision of their buildup, nor in the prudence and wisdom of their juridical prescriptions, nor even in their masterly accommodation of the means employed to the ends sought. The principal value of the *Constitutions* lies in the spirit of the *Exercises* which runs through them and gives life to all their significant elements. Further, the *Constitutions,* which govern the life of each individual Jesuit and that of the whole body of the Society, presuppose men who have made the Exercises in depth and have opted for the most radical expression of the following of Christ: men who are motivated by love. The Exercises are the first 'experience' of the Jesuit at his entrance into the Society—understanding this word 'entrance' in its technical sense, that is, the real verification that his personal call from the Spirit is in accord with the charism of the Society. Hence it is the inner force of the *Exercises* that motivates all his later life, as this is set forth

31 *SpEx,* [370].

organically in the *Constitutions;* hence, too, all renewal of the Society must necessarily entail an effective realization of the vital elements of the Exercises.

14. I hold, however, that two things must be noted when one is tracing a parallel between the *Exercises* and the *Constitutions.*

(a). The individual context in which the *Exercises* are conceived (and which must be preserved when they are made in groups) gives rise to an understanding of love prevalently as a personal relationship between God or Christ the Lord and the exercitant. The love and service of men is implicit—true, as a fundamental and constitutive element—in the love and service of God. But the *Constitutions,* which begin where the *Exercises* leave off, are obviously conceived in a communal and institutionalized form; they are geared to the implementation of that service—'the greater service'—and to the support of men dedicated to that service. As such, they make more explicit the fraternal dimension of charity and love, and the commitment to helping other men—that is, 'our fellowmen' or 'souls' in the vocabulary of Ignatius. The *Constitutions,* or the Society, make effective that trait that the *Exercises* demand of love: self-giving. What in the *Exercises* was a promise of surrender and close following, is in the *Constitutions* reality and action. And all this is brought about by a sharing of ideals and of life with other friends in the Lord, who are joined together by love and a common mission. There is no other law but love. The *Constitutions,* as Ignatius himself terms them in the first paragraph of their Preamble, are no more than the prop and support of reason for "the interior law of charity and love which the Holy Spirit writes and engraves upon hearts."[32] Every Jesuit can in reality and with deep interior joy echo the jubilant words of Paul: "God has qualified me to be minister of a new convenant, not in a written code but in the Spirit; for the written code kills, but the Spirit gives life."[33] This is what Ignatius wants for his *Constitutions:* "No Constitutions, Declarations, or regime of living are to oblige under mortal or venial sin... Thus, in place of the fear of giving offense, there should arise a

32 *Cons,* [134].
33 2 Cor. 3:6.

love and desire of all perfection, and a desire that greater glory and praise of Christ, our Creator and Lord, may follow."[34] In a word, in the Society, one proceeds "in a spirit of love and not troubled by fear."[35]

15. On the personal level, too, for the Jesuit the *Constitutions* begin where the *Exercises* leave off. The ordering of one's life so that no decision is taken under the influence of any inordinate attachment—that is, the goal of the *Exercises*—is presupposed as a starting-point in the *Constitutions*. Hence the Society cannot be built up except of men who live by the spirit of the *Exercises*. In these Exercises, the one who prepares himself to be a Jesuit is brought face to face with himself and with God, and finishes by enlisting under his standard. Once in the Society, he must face the needs of the world and the factual situation of each day, making effective in them his service and his love. But there is a continuity without a break between both stages: God, His love and love for Him are the initial and final cause, the alpha and the omega, of a Jesuit's life-story in the Society. Because of this, for the preservations of "its spirit, and for the attainment of the objective it seeks...the means which unite the human instrument to God...are more effective than those which equip it in relation to men. Such means are, for example, goodness and virtue, and especially charity."[36]

C. Characteristics of Ignatian charity

1. Dynamic love

16. Charity, like every other virtue, aims at growth. But in Ignatius, man of the 'magis', this growth is an insatiable thirst. 'To grow', 'to increase', 'to move ahead' are terms which recur once and again in his writings. 'To grow in His service' is a favorite expression.[37] 'To move ahead' appears again and again in his letters of direction, with the pressing exhortation that it be 'more every

34 *Cons,* [602].
35 *Cons,* [547].
36 *Cons,* [813].
37 *EppIgn,* I, 150.

day', 'from day to day', 'continually', 'even unto perfection'.[38] His eagerness for the progress of his sons is such that, in the *Constitutions,* he goes so far as to suggest to superiors the pedagogy of provocation to encourage the progress of those who are in probation "by testing them" (as he himself might have seen in his youth at Arevalo the bulls for the contest being "tested" to make sure they were of quality breed) "that they may give an example of their virtue and grow in it."[39] But in Ignatius. love is dynamic principally because, as love for God and of men, it leads him to intense activity. All the drive of apostolic service in the Society can be reduced to this concept: love. I shall deal with this later on.

2. *Ordered love*

17. Ordered love, that is to say, love purified of all inordinate attachment to oneself, to persons (relatives, friends) or to things. On this point the *Constitutions* echo exactly the *Exercises*. Ordered love has a negative aspect, to begin with: a refining of love, cleansing it of the dross of inordinate attachment to things for their own sake, in order to love God alone purely, and all other persons and things only in Him and for His sake.[40] In practice, for Ignatius, the purity of love is the purity of intention. He is quite explicit about this when in the *Exercises* he deals with the motives for election: "Let it be noted if the choice has not been made as it should have been, and with due order, that is, if it was not made without inordinate attachments... Since such a choice was inordinate and awry, it does not seem to be a vocation from God... For every vocation that comes from God is always pure and undefiled, uninfluenced by the flesh or any other inordinate attachment."[41] Two paragraphs lower down, he will equate a choice made sincerely with a choice made with due order. The concept is clear, and its motivation too: that a choice be not 'inordinate and awry' but 'pure and

38 See Ignacio Ipparraguirre, S.J., *Vocabulario de Ejercicios Espirituales: Ensava de hermenéutica Ignaciana* (Rome: Iganatian Center of Spirituality, 1972).
39 *Cons,* [285].
40 *Cons,* [288].
41 *SpEx,* [172].

undefiled', "the love that moves and causes one to choose must descend from above, that is, from the love of God."[42]

18. The passage in the *Constitutions* that is parallel to this one concerning choice which we have just considered in the *Exercises,* is that regarding the renunciation of goods, which one who enters the Society should be ready to make. The 'ordering' of one's affections is here required with special emphasis. One should "put aside all merely natural affection for his relatives and convert it into spiritual, by loving them only with that love which rightly ordered charity requires."[43] At the moment of relinquishing these goods, one should divest oneself of disordered love of relatives, to avoid the disadvantage of a disordered distribution which proceeds from that aforementioned love."[44] This renunciation could be required of one even at the end of the first year of novitiate, if it is judged that putting it off might be the occasion in a particular novice for "disorder arising from his placing some love and confidence in it" (his property).[45] For poverty is a specially critical area, a genuine test-case for the 'purity' and 'ordered' character of our love. In the Society, therefore, we must come to a "total contempt of temporal things, in regard to which self-love frequently induces disorder."[46]

19. Another area that is open to 'disorder', and therefore deserves special watchfulness, is that of 'sensuality' or self-love. Hence, when dealing with it, Ignatius is once again especially explicit. When the Jesuit, at the end of his studies, is about to be admitted to profession, a final check must be carried out on this point. He is made to pass from the school of the intellect to "the school of the heart, by exercising himself in spiritual and corporal pursuits which can engender in him greater humility, abnegation of all sensual love and will and judgment of his own, and also greater knowledge and love of God our Lord."[47] It is the final ordering of love, the definitive clarification needed for the apostolic mission

42 *SpEx,* [184].
43 *Cons,* [61].
44 *Cons,* [54].
45 *Cons,* [254].
46 *Cons,* [671].
47 *Cons,* [516].

given by the Society. He will thus realize in himself that ideal regarding love which was held out to him at his entrance into the Society: "to abhor in its totality and not in part whatever the world loves and embraces...to accept and desire with all possible energy whatever Christ our Lord loved and embraced... Those, who are truly following Christ our Lord, love and intensely desire everything opposite to that which men of the world love and seek with such great diligence."[48] This is the golden rule of 'ordered love'. The *Constitutions* are written in this perspective and for men who live this ideal, or desire to live it, or at least "wish to have holy desires of this kind."[49]

3. *Discerning love* (discreta caritas)

20. Discretion adds to ordered love an important and typically Ignatian trait: sound judgment. It does away with excess, the *hubris* of the Greeks; it excludes wild and rash haste, the exaggerations of ardent apostolic zeal, those secondary effects that make love itself counter-productive. But discretion does not mean putting limits to love. The love of God is infinite, and man' response to it is to be "with all your heart, with all your soul and with all your strength."[50] Discretion in love is a complement to 'order', and hence a condition for growth. Ignatius is temperamentally a secondary type, a reflexive type. His education at court and military training have endowed him with remarkable self-control and with a sense of the limits of his own resources. Discretion in love is the rational counterpoise that balances off the affective and makes it fully human. It is that measure of supernatural prudence, of the proportion between means and ends, of respect for the person with his or her circumstances, that makes it possible for ordered love to achieve its objectives while having due regard for a well-graded scale of values.

21. Here are some examples. Ignatius requires of us special care and caution at the moment of admitting someone to the Society.

48 *Cons,* [101].
49 *Cons,* [102].
50 Luke, 10:27.

The one who admits "should be vigilant that charity for an individual does not impair the charity for all, which should always be preferred."[51] The same discretion must prevent us from keeping in the Society one who is not suitable: we should not "retain someone...contrary to the good of the Society. Since this is a universal good, it ought to be preferred to the good of one individual... To tolerate this would be attributable not to charity but to its very opposite."[52] It would be "indiscreet charity in retaining him who is useless or harmful to the Society."[53] If a cause suffices or not for dismissal, it is the "discreet charity of the superior..." that "ought to ponder it before God our Lord."[54] When dealing with the Professed, discretion is even more clearly emphasized, for in their case "the charity and discretion of the Holy Spirit will indicate the manner which ought to be used."[55] "Well-ordered and discreet charity" will dictate the manner of dealing with those who abandon the Society and take the habit in another religious institute,[56] dictate too the penances that may be imposed,[57] and the amount of time which the Professed and Formed Coadjutors are to give to prayer or to study.[58] Discerning love, finally, is that "prudent charity" with which Ignatius supposes the General of the Society to be endowed.[59]

4. Love that permeates everything

22. Every single page of the *Constitutions* is written in terms of charity or love, be this explicitly so, or in the equivalent terms of the service of God or the glory of God. These are different formal aspects of one and the same reality: the surrender, in a return of love for love, to the Father's work—to which Ignatius was admitted at La Storta—with Christ, by the grace of the Spirit. The men-

---

51 *Cons,* [189].
52 *Cons,* [212].
53 *Cons,* [217].
54 *Cons,* [209].
55 *Cons,* [219].
56 *Cons,* [237].
57 *Cons,* [269].
58 *Cons,* [582].
59 *Cons,* [754].

tal discipline with which the *Constitutions* are conceived, the power of effectiveness that they embody, the juridical precision—exceptional for their day—with which they are formulated, do not conceal from those who read or study them with an open mind what lies much deeper: an absolute loyalty, born of whole-hearted love, to the mission received and towards the giver of that mission. And, in order to fulfill that mission, a wondrous harmonizing of two apparently contrary elements: a strong system of monarchical authority exercised through a government which is, above all, fatherly, or based on love.

23. The entire life of a Jesuit should be inspired by charity and love. From the moment when, soon after his entrance into the Society, he finds himself deliberately put in conditions in which he must "with genuine faith and intense love place his reliance entirely in his Creator and Lord"[60] until he dies, striving to give an "example of...living faith, hope, and love of the eternal goods...with help from fraternal charity."[61] Towards God, his life will be "love and reverence"; towards his brothers, "fraternal charity".[62] As regards superiors, "from their hearts they should warmly love them as fathers in Jesus Christ." "Thus in everything they should proceed in a spirit of charity."[63] And, portraying himself without intending to do so, Ignatius exhorts the General never to "cease to have proper sympathy for his sons."[64]

24. Love or charity is, for Ignatius, a basic component of all the virtues. Poverty is not merely accepted; it is chosen out of love for the poor Christ. The same with humility. Love is the soul of obedience;[65] it is present in all the various degrees of the correction which the Superior is to give with discerning love: "the first time, with love and sweetness; the second time, with love and also in such a way that they feel humiliating shame; the third time, with love but

60 *Cons*, [67].
61 *Cons*, [595].
62 *Cons*, [273, 280, 595].
63 *Cons*, [551].
64 *Cons*, [727].
65 *Cons*, [547, 551].

in such a way that they have fear."[66] Love, together with reverence, is the profound justification for the indifference towards the grades with which one enters the Society.[67] It is out of love that studies are taken up.[68] Finally it is love and charity that are highlighted in that "great probity and love of the Society" which should not be wanting in the General even if he should lack other qualities,[69] leading him even so far as "to receive death, if necessary, for the good of the Society in the service of Jesus Christ, God and our Lord."[70] We have here one of the most solemn formulas employed by Ignatius.

5. Love, source of union

25. Speaking to Jesuits, I am obliged to dwell on an effect of mutual love that is fundamental for Ignatius: union. Union is a primordial value in the Society, the condition for its survival, because it is union that makes the Society's being a 'body' compatible with our mission for dispersal. So important is this for Ignatius that to it he dedicates one whole part of the ten parts of the *Constitutions,* Part VIII: "Helps towards uniting the dispersed members with their head and among themselves." The first section of this Part VIII deals precisely with "the union of minds and hearts." On the exterior level, the first measure—together with obedience and authority—is selection in admissions. This is precisely the topic which in the second part of the *Constitutions* evokes the greatest number of references to discretion in charity. But then, this is not the point which most concerns us now. Nevertheless, it is curious to remark that in the 'autograph' copy of the *Constitutions,* paragraph 667b—in which the exercise of authority is tempered with graciousness and gentleness—there is a manuscript addition made by Ignatius: "having his method of commanding well thought out and organized...that the Superior on his part uses all the love and modesty and charity possible in our Lord, so that the subjects can dispose themselves to have always towards their superiors greater love than fear."

66 *Cons,* [270].
67 *Cons,* [111, 130].
68 *Cons,* [361].
69 *Cons,* [735].
70 *Cons,* [728].

26. However, it is not juridical means that will provide the type of union that the Society needs. For there is question, in the first place, of 'uniting minds and hearts' in order to unite the body, and for this "the chief bond to cement the union of the members among themselves and with their head is, on both sides, the love of God our Lord. For when the Superior and the subjects are closely united to His Divine and Supreme Goodness, they will very easily be united among themselves, through that same love which will descend from the Divine Goodness and spread to all other men, and particularly into the body of the Society."[71] Once again, Ignatius returns to his favorite conception: the descent of the love of God and its diffusion, through us, to all our fellowmen, first among whom are the very members of the Society. Ignatius is not afraid of repeating himself, and so he adds: "Thus from both sides charity will come to further this union, and in general all goodness and virtues through which one proceeds in conformity with the spirit." Ignatius is convinced that if we respond to the love of Christ with the love for Christ, there will necessarily spring up among us mutual love. To preserve its union the Society does not rely on other means which the monastic orders can freely use, such as work and prayer in common and a strict living together in community. In the Society union must have bonds which somehow go beyond all this, because they must be compatible with dispersion and, in fact, give meaning to this dispersion. Such bonds 'ad intra' are charity and mutual love, intimately felt and deeply at work; 'ad extra', the sharing in a worldwide mission through personal mission. All this will be further helped by the possible uniformity of views and by frequent communication among the scattered members. For Ignatius this union of minds and hearts is of such value that he reserves some of the hardest words of all the *Constitutions* for those who cause it harm, urging that such persons "ought with great diligence to be separated from that community as a pestilence,"[72] even perhaps expelled from the Society.

27. Ignatius led the way by his own example of love and charity towards all. The anecdotal history of Ignatian charity is vast,

71 *Cons,* [671].
72 *Cons,* [664].

spread over the pages of the volumes of Monumenta: charity, true love of a father, towards the novices, the sick and ailing, those undergoing trials. I need hardly dwell on what is sufficiently known to all. But I do think it helpful to mention what he wrote to Father Melchior Carneiro who had been appointed Bishop for the Ethiopian mission, since it gives us the Ignatian formulation of the theory of union: "Hold it for certain that...we will always keep you close to our hearts, drawing you all the more closely in an interior union as you are farther removed from our exterior presence."[73] In the case of Father Godinho, who was having a difficult time, he offers this assurance: "I hold you very close to my heart."[74] Father Luis Goncalves da Camara, Ignatius's confidant for the Autobiography, left this portrait of him in the Memoriale which he wrote during the lifetime of Ignatius: "He is always more inclined to love, so much so indeed, that everything in him appears to be love."[75]

28. The ideal of remaining 'united in love while being scattered' is exemplified in a singular manner by him who was the farthest of the scattered brethren, Francis Xavier. This impetuous Navarrese, lost in the remoteness of another world, feels himself united with the whole Society by a love which he expresses in such affectively-charged phrases, which recur so often, that they seem unlikely in a man of his capacity for action. Xavier insists he is "absent only bodily, but present in spirit."[76] All of the teaching on union and dispersal is contained in this phrase of Xavier's: "God who in His mercy joined us together, and for His service separated us...."[77] Of the letters which he receives, Xavier cuts pieces with the signatures of his companions and carries them with him; he writes to St. Ignatius "kneeling on the floor, as if I had you present before me."[78] He writes "to my Father Ignatius, and to the rest of my brother in, this most beloved Society of Jesus, who live in Rome or in any

73 Letter of Feb. 26, 1555, in *EppIgn,* VIII, 489-490; *LettersIgn,* p. 374.
74 Letter of Jan. 31, 1552, in *EppIgn,* IV, 126; *LettersIgn,* p. 254.
75 Luis Goncalves da Câmara, *Memoriale,* no. 86, in *FN.* I, 579.
76 Letter of March 18, 1541 from Lisbon, in *Epistolae S. Francisci Xaverii* (2 vols in MHSJ, hereafter abbreviated *EppXav*), I, 78.
77 Letter of Jan. 15, 1544, from Cochin, in *EppXav,* I, 176.
78 Cochin, Jan. 12, 1549, in *EppXav,* II, 16.

body or exterior of the Society, but also of its spirit, and for the attainment of the objective it seeks."[84] The whole of the Tenth Part of the *Constitutions* is dedicated to this subject. Among the means that will ensure the preservation and growth of the Society is mentioned *especially charity*."[85] This ideal, in the very last pages of the *Constitutions,* ties up perfectly with the very first number of their Preamble, in which it is acknowledged that it is the Supreme Goodness of God that will preserve, direct, and carry forward the Society, and that our cooperation with it is to be through the interior law of charity and love. Thus is closed the circle of the *Constitutions* with an exaltation of charity and love, in the same way that the *Exercises* begin by purifying man in the attachments of his heart and culminate in an exaltation of love. It could not be otherwise. As Nadal wrote in his "Commentary on the Institute": "This law of love, engraved on our hearts, helps beyond measure in the preservation and growth of the Society. No other spirit, but this one of charity and love, inspired the birth of the Society."[86]

7. Apostolic love

31. If, when treating of Ignatius' intimacy with the Trinity, we saw that his was a mysticism which led him to apostolic action, we must now say the same regarding his charity. The charity and love of Ignatius translates itself into apostolic zeal. But it is not of this zeal as such that I wish to speak, but of the basis of this zeal: namely, of the explicit and precise reality of love felt for men, of a love directed to 'one's fellowmen'. Ignatius' love takes its starting-point from his desire that all men should know the infinite love of God and respond to it. In this consists the spread of the Kingdom and the return of all things to the Father. Ignatius loves God in men, and men in God. The Society which he founds on these bases has no other motive force than that which it can get from an ardent charity.

8. Love, the objective of the Society

31. Love in action, universal love, love without limits, whether

---

84 *Cons,* [813].
85 Ibid.
86 Nadal, Exhortations of 1554 in Spain, *MonNad, V, 83.*

in space or in kind or in the means it employs, is, we might say, what specifies the Society among the religious institutes of contemplative or mixed life, with which it has in common the desire for the salvation and perfection of 'our own souls' and of the neighbor. Elsewhere[87] I have emphasized that Nadal was keen that Jesuits should be quite clear on this point. Without this apostolic extension of our charity and love, the foundation of the Society would not be justified. "We do not place the perfection of our state in contemplation or in prayer as if they were the only means with which to help our fellowmen, while we remain closed up in our rooms or cells. The perfection of the monastic orders does certainly consist in this; as for us, charity urges us on."[88] And even more explicitly: "The heavenly Father has given to the Society as its goal and objective the fullness and perfection of charity."[89]

33. Nadal gets enthusiastic when he deals with this subject, notably wherever and to whomsoever he explains the *Constitutions*. To have clearly fixed in the minds and hearts of Jesuits the sublimity of the Society's goal was fundamental, if they were to identify themselves with its authentic spirit. Nadal's sheer delight is evident when he affirms over and over again that "the objective of the Society is the same as that of Christ.[90] The goal given us is the most perfect possible, that is, the very same which the heavenly Father assigned to His only Son in His incarnation, in His life, death, and resurrection...the salvation and perfection of souls achieved through full and perfect charity."[91] Nadal's enthusiasm knows no limits: "What do you think is the perfection we seek? It is not poverty, nor chastity, nor obedience."[92] He said the same to the Jesuit students of Cologne: "Our aim is not poverty, chastity or obedience, but charity and its perfection or, in other words, the greater glory of God and the love of our fellowmen. Poverty, etc.,

---

87 Trinitarian Inspiration of the Ignatian Charism, no. 77, in *ActRSJ*, XVIII, 148-149.

88 Nadal, Annotations of 1557 on the *Examen*, [16], in *MonNad*, V, 140.

89 Ibid, [17].

90 Nadal, Exhortations of 1554 in Spain, [118], *MonNad*, V, 83-84.

91 Nadal, Annotations on the *Examen*, [14], *MonNad*, V, 139.

92 Nadal, Exhortations of 1561 at Alcalá, [90], *MonNad*, V, 333.

are no more than means."[93] Finally, sober Majorcan though Nadal is, he gets carried away, as it were, into literary flights that are not his usual style: "This referring all to the love of God or the greater glory of God is a most perfect goal. This is absolutely clear in all the *Constitutions*. Others do all for the glory of God; we, for His greater glory. It is like being on fire"![94] What a splendid literary phrase! This should not, however, surprise us: Ignatius himself, about whose literary style everybody feels competent to express a sort of superior smile, does achieve a happy turn of phrase at least on one occasion when, seeking to encourage an administrator who was hankering after priestly ministries, he assures him that that work, accepted in obedience, could be as valuable as contemplation and "even more acceptable to Him, proceeding as it does from a more powerful and vigorous charity."[95]

9. Love that assists even materially

34. Love for our fellowmen is exercised primarily in procuring their spiritual good through means that are specifically spiritual. The Formula of the Institute, no. 3, and the *Constitutions* are diaphanously clear on this point. It is a consequence of the essentially priestly character of the Society. But the corporal works of mercy are also included "to the extent that the more important spiritual ones permit."[96] It is the General's "discretion" that should regulate the distribution of the "forces" of the Society; "he should always keep the greater service of God and the more universal good before his eyes." Such a balance should take into account the three pairs of values that Ignatius highlights when he lists his criteria for the selection of ministries: "benefits for the soul— benefits for the body; matters pertaining to their greater perfection—to their lesser perfection; things which are in themselves of more good—of less good. In all these cases, the first should be preferred to the second."[97]

93 Nadal, Exhortations of 1567 at Cologne, [29], in *MonNad*. V, 791.
94 Ibid., [13], *MonNad* V, 785.
95 Letter of Jan 31, 1552 from Rome to Manuel Godinho, in *EppIgn*, IV, 126; *LettersIgn*, p. 255.
96 *Cons*, [650].
97 *Cons*, [623].

35. Nadal, when explaining the Institute, developed this point in the following way. "To sum up: nothing that charity can do to help the neighbor is excluded from our Institute, provided that all our service (*omnia ministeria*) is seen to be spiritual, and that we are quite clear on the point that the service proper to us is the more perfect one, namely, the purely spiritual ministries. We should not take up others that are in themselves lower except through necessity, after having given much thought to the question, with much hope and great fruit, and with the permission of Superiors; and, finally, when service in the purely spiritual field is not feasible."[98]

36. But the fact that a particular ministry is spiritual is not an absolute criterion to make it capable of being exercised out of charity. Ignatius excludes some such ministries explicitly when he treats of "the occupations which those in the Society should or should not undertake."[99] However, we must never forget the reservation globally embracing the priorities of choice that is presumed by the clause *caeteris paribus,* "when other considerations are equal," which is repeated twice over (nos. 622 and 623), and with the addition in one case that it applies to everything that follows. Nor must we overlook the importance given in these criteria for the choice of ministries to the urgency and emergency of a situation, which would then demand priority of attention. Natural calamities and disasters—like outbreaks of famine, epidemics, catastrophes—make demands on our charity for assistance and help that can brook no delay.

10. The Example of Ignatius

37. The practical conduct of Ignatius in this matter is of a decisively instructive value for us. His action as General is the irreplaceable "practical implementation' of the *Constitutions* that we must make our own. Ignatius teaches us by his deeds the primacy that charity—even initiatives of material assistance—can and must have, in given circumstances, in the totality of the Society's apostolic activity.

---

98 Nadal, Annotations on the *Examen,* [20], in *MonNad,* V, 141.
99 *Cons,* [582].

Aid to the famine stricken. The winter of 1538—the second winter for the first companions in Rome—has gone down in history as "the winter of famine." People were living in a situation of emergency. The harvest had all but failed. Ignatius' own problems were gigantic. The campaign of defamation let loose by his slanderers threatened to ruin his whole work of founding the Society, so that he had to spend entire days in the official lobbies and the courts until he obtained a sentence of acquittal on November 18th. He had yet another problem to face. Precisely at this time there elapsed the year of waiting to which Ignatius and his companions had bound themselves by the vow of making a pilgrimage to Jerusalem, with the result that they were all deeply taken up with concern for their future. It is during this week, running from 18th to 23rd of November, that they take the decisive step of presenting themselves to Paul III. As if all this were not enough, Ignatius was busy, on a personal level, with a matter of the greatest importance, the celebration of his First Mass, since the reason for its delay had disappeared with the cancellation of the voyage to Jerusalem. Can we really imagine the spiritual earnestness with which Ignatius prepared himself for this fresh encounter with Christ? These, then, were the circumstances in which he and his nine companions gave themselves totally to the assistance of the famine-stricken of Rome. So intense and profound was this experience that all the early historical sources of the Society dwell on its details when reporting it.[100] Ignatius and his companions would set out at early dawn from their new residence—the house of Antonio Frangipani, next to the Tower of Melangolo—to beg for bread, wood, and straw to lie on; then they would carry it all on their shoulders to their poor apartments. Going out again, they would gather the beggars and starving people, who literally lay in the slush of the streets of Rome, bring them together, and make them comfortable as best they could—some 400 of them at a time—or offer them some ration of food. Thus they were able to help more than 3,000 persons in a city which then counted scarcely 40,000 inhabitants.[101]

100 Laínez, Polanco, Simáo Rodrigues, and others (see *FN*, I, 126, 199, etc.), and
       Ignatius himself, in *EppIgn*, I, 218.
101 Tacchi Venturi, *Storia della Compagnia di Gesù*, II/1, 166.

38. *Aid to the oppressed and exploited groups.* Ignatius is not satisfied with a charity that offers material assistance merely on an individual basis. His inner vision leads him to discover the collective sad plight of very definite social groups. His charity drives him to make every effort to obtain for them a more just treatment at the hands of social structures.

(a). *The Jews* were numerous in Rome; its Jewish quarter was full of both wealthy and miserable Jews. Not a few of them got themselves baptized through conviction, convenience, or pressure. They were subjected to injustice inasmuch as, at the moment of baptism, they were required to renounce all their goods and turn them over to the official treasury as a sign of their total break with the past. Such exploitation not only made conversions difficult or altogether prevented them; it was legalized robbery. Ignatius worked, appealed, moved influential persons and succeeded in getting Paul III in March 1542 to issue the Brief *Cupientes Judaeos,* which allowed baptized Jews to retain their possessions.

But for Ignatius, this was not sufficient. Overcoming all the prejudices of the times, he protected and helped these Jews personally as much as he could. He started gathering them together in his own Curia adjoining the Chapel of Santa Maria della Strada, and later obtained from a person he was directing spiritually—"Madama Margarita," daughter of the Emperor Charles—the foundation of separate asylums for converted Jews and Jewesses. Ignatius gives an account of this to Xavier in a letter that is full of joy, and adds: "We distributed among the new converts all the beds and furniture we had in the house, and the alms too we set aside and stored up for the same purpose. Seeing that this work is so well ordered, and confirmed by apostolic authority, we hope in our Lord to move on to others."[102] Such was the charity of Ignatius. He and his companions, living in the overcrowded house of la Strada, could not have had an excess of household furniture in it; yet he gave it all. When a field that he has tilled begins to bear abundant fruit, Ignatius hands it over to others, so he can dedicate himself to breaking new ground. Such was his system, such his conception of assistance and help.

---

102 *EppIgn,* I, 269.

39. (b). *The beggars.* Beggary had been banned in Rome. There as in other places, then as now, it was a social scourge in which authentic need got mixed up with shrewd swindling. But an indiscriminate ban had succeeded in further aggravating the sorry plight of the truly poor of those days when there was no social security, unemployment subsidy, or old-age pension. The poor and the sick, the old and the crippled filled the streets of Rome. Ignatius assisted those that he could; for all, he obtained from the pope the Brief *Dudum per Nos* (1542), which mitigated the ban and established the Society of Orphans, which was to be charged with the task of sifting "the poor who were sick or crippled in any way" from those "able-bodied" others that were capable of doing work.

40. (c). *The courtesans.* A class that was at once exploited, maintained, and despised by a hypocritical society. To them, too, Ignatius directs his charity, to free them as a group from the unjust structure that oppressed them. There were already other institutions that were helping them. But it was unjust that such institutions accepted only those who agreed to spend the rest of their lives as penitents in a religious order. Ignatius rejected this as making it difficult and painful for these women to change their lives; he contended that this was in effect coercion, against the freedom of the person. He founded his own work, that of St. Martha, to which he admitted not only those who wished to enter religion as penitents, but also others, married women and spinsters, particularly those who were known in Rome as "reputable courtesans," frequented by the nobility. All these were helped by Ignatius until some definitive solution was found for them: either rejoining their husbands, or marriage for the spinsters, or religious life, or some decent position. "A charming sight"—writes Ribadeneira—"to see this holy old man walking ahead of one of those unfortunate women, still young and good-looking, as it were making way and opening a path for her."[103] In keeping with his way of doing things, Ignatius also established a pious association—the Society of Grace—to see that that work of St. Martha was carried on, and obtained its canonical erection by means of the Bull of the 16th of

---

103 Ribadeneira, *De actis P.N. Ignatii,* in *FN,* II, 346.

February, 1543. From his own poor resources Ignatius drew money to finance the new institution, but at what great cost and with what trouble! His house of Santa Maria della Strada was full to overflowing with Jesuits, and money was scarce. And yet, when his administrator Codacio discovered in the wooded clearing of Sant' Andrea de la Fracta huge blocks of stone and marble, remains of Roman monuments, Ignatius had yet another burst and impulse of charity: "Sell those stones that you have removed, and from them obtain for me a sum amounting to one hundred ducats."[104] That considerable amount was all for the house of St. Martha—and this, let us never forget, in the financial circumstances in which Ignatius was!

41. (d). *Young women in danger.* Scarcely had he handed over to others the work of St. Martha, when Ignatius, in his characteristic way, embarked on another: the *Compagnia delle Vergini miserabili,* the Association of Hapless Young Women—a work of prevention, of social protection of women, we might say today. Ignatius encouraged wealthy and charitable persons to enrol in it, and obtained pontifical approval for it. Similarly he established a group of twelve trustworthy men through whose good offices he distributed help to those ashamed to identify themselves as poor. With it was born the Society of the Most Blessed Sacrament, under the supervision of the General of the Society of Jesus.

42. I ask myself what would have been Ignatius's attitude today in the face of the calamities of our times: the boat-people, the starving thousands in the Sahara belt, the refugees and forced migrants of today. What would have been his attitude in the face of the suffering of such clearly defined groups of victims of criminal exploitation, as are, for example, the drug-addicts? Would we be mistaken in thinking that Ignatius, in our times, would have done more than we are doing, that he would have acted in a way different from us?

11. Ignatius' own experience of charity

43. Ignatius had arrived at this intelligent practice of charity by two routes: by the roads of personal experience and by that of

104 Ribadeneira, *Vida de N. P. San Ignacio,* in *FN,* IV, 411.

spiritual choice. Ignatius had been poor, voluntarily poor, painfully poor, a real beggar. He had learned to value charity in his own personal experience of need. He walked the streets of Manresa, **Barcelona, Alcalá, Salamanca, and Paris; he wandered through the** ports of Barcelona, Haifa, and Gaeta; he traversed the routes of Flanders and England, begging only to eat poorly. He gave up the remnants of his alms when he felt the need to surrender more completely into the provident hands of God. If at times during his studies he kept the donations given him, it was out of a firm conviction of an "ordered and discerning love" directed towards himself. But, already in 1536, he wrote that his desire was to remain always in such a condition as "to preach as a poor man, and certainly not with the embarrassing abundance I now enjoy by reason of my studies. However that may be, as a pledge of what I here say, I am going to send you, when my studies are finished, the few books I now have, or may have then."[105] Ignatius had experienced the value of the charity of others in his own poverty. When General of the Society, he poured out his own love and charity most generously onto the poverty of others.

44. It is not at all surprising, therefore, that charity is a constant point of reference in Ignatius's spiritual teaching. I shall say nothing here of charity as a spiritual option, such as it is presented in the *Exercises* or institutionalized in the *Constitutions*. But I must refer, even if only in passing, to the place occupied by charity in Ignatius' letters. In the letters addressed to his relatives in Loyola or to his benefactors in Barcelona, to his protectors or simply to those whom he directed spiritually—persons of great rank or of lowly condition—to the Jesuits scattered over Europe or Asia, in all these letters a prominent place is repeatedly given to almsgiving, visits to hospitals and prisons, assistance to those in need. This type of recommendation is, of course, never missing in the instructions with which Ignatius sends someone on a 'mission'—be that to Trent, Germany, England, or Sicily—or for the founding of houses or of colleges. Indeed, it would seem that for Ignatius no ministry or service, be it ever so spiritual in itself, could be deemed com-

---

105 Letter of Feb. 12, 1536 from Venice to Jaime Cassador, *EppIgn*, I, 93-99; *LettersIgn*, p. 16.

plete were it not complemented by the charitable works of material assistance. And vice versa. For it is clear that, for Ignatius, the true exercise of love for one's fellowmen is apostolic zeal, the ardent desire to procure his salvation and perfection; but it is no less evident that Ignatius loves man whole and entire, as did the Lord for whose sake alone he loves.

II. THE ROOT AND FOUNDATION

A. *One single object of charity*

45. Ignatius had succeeded in perfectly unifying his love of God, a "most intense love directed totally to loving the Most Holy Trinity,"[106] with love for his fellow men. This is the model of charity that the *Exercises* and the *Constitutions* ask of us, the integration of charity that Paul, the apostle of service to the neighbor, and John, the apostle of love of God, proclaimed and lived.

Paul, like Ignatius, was a convert, passionately dedicated to Christ, to whom he showed his love by an intense service in the defense and spread of the faith. Very few are the times, though, when he mentions that love explicitly in his letters. He uses other expressions instead: living for Christ, walking towards Christ, anathema on anyone who does not love Christ, and the like. Yet his love impelled him to serve his brothers, whom he loved as intensely as he loved Christ. This tension becomes evident in one of his most beautiful texts: "I am caught in this dilemma: I want to be gone and be with Christ, which would be very much the better, but for me to stay alive in this body is a more urgent need for your sake."[107] Paul is sure that he will continue to live with them. For if, as he tells the Corinthians, he feels the overwhelming drive of the love of Christ, it is precisely because he realizes that Christ has died for all, "so that living men should live no longer for themselves, but for him who died and was raised to life for them."[108] Moreover, his love for Christ contains an apostolic thrust, and thus the best way Paul knows to satisfy his thirst for identification with

106 See *Spiritual Dairy,* [106-108], entries of March 4, 1544.
107 Phil. 1:23.
108 2 Cor. 5:14.

Christ is by devoting himself to the service of men, concretely of the 'gentiles.' This service is owed to all men, inasmuch as in every man, notably in the weaker ones, there is a "brother for whom Christ dies."[109]

46. John's teaching is identical, but in a more explicitly Trinitarian framework, because for him the relationship among the Father, the Word and men is more explicit: "God loved the world so much that he gave his only Son, so that everyone who believes in him may not be lost but may have eternal life."[110] This insertion of men into the heart of divine love takes place radically in the very bosom of the Trinity: "The Father loves me because I lay down my life"[111] and "the Father himself loves you for loving me."[112] John keeps coming back to this idea: "Anybody who loves me will be loved by my Father,"[113] he comes to it from many different angles: "As the Father has loved me, so I have loved you."[114] Moreover, this same John who so clearly states the love relationship among the Father, the Son, and every man adds to it our charity—love for our brothers—which is the commandment that Jesus calls "mine" and "new." Christ, who set the commandment of brotherly love alongside the first commandment of loving God,[115] seems to invert the terms: we must love our brothers so that we can say that we love God. We love our neighbor, nor only as Christ loved us, but because Christ loved us; and it is by loving our neighbor that we love Christ and the Father. John explains this in the words of Jesus: He leaves the world, but yet remains in each one of us. Hence we must remain united, since his presence links us together. We must be 'one' as he and the Father are one.[116] This union through love will be the witness by which the world will come to believe that the Son has been sent.[117] Reading this text of John, a Jesuit cannot fail

---

109 1 Cor. 8:11.
110 John 3:16; see also 10:15, 17:30.
111 John 10:17.
112 John 16:27.
113 John 14:21.
114 John 15:9.
115 Matt. 22:39.
116 John 17:11.
117 John 17:21-23.

to be reminded of the Society's urgent call to mutual love so that it can remain united and fulfill its mission. There is no better comment on that text than of our *Constitutions,* [671].

47. In the first of his letters John dwells on the inseparableness of love of God from love of neighbor, understanding love-charity in its operative aspect as gift of self and sharing. The theological root—the "root and foundation," in Paul's metaphor—is the very divine essence: "God is love."[118] So absolutely is he love that "love comes from God and...anyone who fails to love can never have known God." A love that consists in the giving of self, the supreme evidence of which was given when the Father sent "his Son to be the sacrifice that takes our sins away." Immediately John draws the consequences of this: "Since God has loved us so much, we too should love one another. And then his final conclusion: "As long as we love one another God will live in us and his love will be complete in us."[119] God the Father wanted it this way because so it had to be. Neither the love that is in him, nor the love that he has put into man, can be broken up into separate parts. It is a drive that is total and indivisible in man just as it is one in God. We love God because he gave us his Son, we love our brothers because the Son gave himself for them and is in them. Responding to the Father's love with our love for our brothers, we share in the divine life that is love.

48. This brotherly communion of mutual love in Christ is 'koinonia', that shared attitude of brotherly service which shows itself in deeds. In the Society, this 'koinonia' issuing from fraternal love constitutes the totality of our mission to help men to 'believe'—in the Johannine sense of a proclamation of the faith and a dedication to Christ—by spreading the faith, and to help them to love one another by promoting justice among them. Brotherly love is an expression of our divine sonship: "Whoever loves the Father that begot him loves the child whom he begets. We can be sure that we love God's children if we love God himself and do what he has commanded us."[120] We cannot love God cut off from others, nor

118 1 John 4:8.
119 1 John 4:12.
120 1 John 5:1.

in the abstract. It is a trilateral love. To love our brothers, and to show this love in our actions, is not something adventitious, something added to our love of God to complete it. It is a constitutive element demanded by the very notion of the love of God.

49. But we must make the converse statement too: By the very fact that we are Christians, we cannot genuinely love men unless we love God. What is asked of us is not a love of 'philanthropy', but a 'philadelphia', a love of brotherhood. In every man, with all his concrete circumstances, there is a value that does not depend on me, but that makes him like me. God is within him, with his love, waiting for me, and this is a call that I cannot neglect. To refuse love—and the service that goes with love—even to a single person is to refuse to recognize his dignity and, at the same time, to abdicate my own, which has no better foundation than his. It is most important to keep clearly in mind this equality of dignity between each of us and our fellow men, if we are to grasp the viciousness there is in hatred, abuse of the freedom of others, exploitation, in a word, in lack of mercy. 'Anomia'—contempt for and generalized violation of law, the predominance of selfishness—has its clearest condemnation in 'agape', that disinterested and active love which should reign among men. In the unavoidable clash of interests at the heart of our complex human relations, only the values that unify us all can resolve the conflict; we have to accept that even the most solidly founded rights of some must at times yield to the needs of others. God receives in others the love we have for him, and he accepts and cherishes as a service the sacrifice of what we have been given as his sons, but yield in the name of brotherhood. The presence of each man in my life becomes, transcendentally, a form of the presence of God, and my acceptance of my brother becomes my implicit acceptance of God. This is what someone has called the "sacrament of our neighbor."[121]

B. Charity and faith

50. God's love for man precedes our faith and does not depend on it. "What proves that God loves us is that Christ died for us

121 See Juan Alfaro, *Cristología y Antropología* (Madrid, 1973).

while we were still sinners.''[122] In us, on the other hand, theological charity presupposes faith, and only in charity does faith reach its fullness. ''In Christ Jesus whether you are circumcised or not makes no difference—what matters is faith that makes its power felt through love.''[123] Faith gives meaning to our charity, while charity activates and animates our faith. When Christ stimulates our faith in him and in the Father so that we will 'know', he is asking of us not merely a witness-statement or an acknowledgment, but an acceptance of his identity as the One Sent and as the Son, an acceptance of his message of conversion; he is asking us to keep his commandments,[124] especially the new commandment, his own commandment. To us Jesuits, once again, this is all quite familiar: Doesn't it remind us of the Ignatian rhythm in three movements: ''an interior knowledge of the Lord—in order to love him more—and to follow him''? Ignatius's 'interior knowledge' is no different from the 'faith', the 'believing', the 'knowing' that John speaks of; and it leads inexorably to action and to service, as it does in John. This is the real meaning of the assertion that the Jesuit has to be a *homo serviens,* a man given to the service of God and to the service of his brothers.

51. Let me go back to the similarity between all this and Paul's spiritual experience. Paul said: ''The life I now live in this body I live in faith: faith in the Son of God who loved me and who sacrificed himself for my sake.''[125] It is a faith that, as Paul goes on to say, is shown in action by charity. Paul would have felt himself a traitor to the faith he received along the road to Damascus, had he not put it at the service of his mission. For faith bears within itself the seed of mission. Such was the case of Abraham. And, in its own way, the case of Ignatius. For them, works born of faith are part of a divine purpose issuing from on high. To the extent of the grace that is given to each individual, they are also the purpose of the faith that is given him. This is how Paul understood it: ''We pray continually that God will...by his power fulfill all your desires for

122 Rom. 5:8.
123 Gal. 5:6.
124 1 John 5:2-3.
125 Gal. 2:20.

142

goodness and complete all that you have been doing through faith."[126] The vitality of faith, its power for good when animated by charity, is one of the arguments he uses most frequently and vigorously for carrying out "the designs of God which are revealed in faith. The only purpose of this instruction is that there should be love, coming out of a pure heart, a clear conscience and a sincere faith."[127] We find the same juxtaposition of faith and charity in the letter to Philemon: "I hear of the love and the faith which you have for the Lord Jesus and for all the saints. I pray that this faith will give rise to a sense of fellowship."[128]

52. John's teaching is no different. The two loves, which for him are inseparable—the love of God and the love of our brothers—are born of faith. Faith is an integral part of the Father's 'commandments': "His commandments are these: that we believe in the name of his Son Jesus Christ and that we love one another, as he told us to."[129] For John, believing means knowing; it means entering into Christ and sharing in his life, his action and his message. At the same time it means letting oneself be penetrated by Christ. Thus faith, according to John, necessarily calls for love and the works of love, the works of charity: "Everybody who loves is begotten by God and knows God. He who does not love does not know God."[130] John is convinced that faith and charity are inseparable.

We can say the same about the apostle James too. In a style more dramatic than epistolary, he succeeds in devising a dialogue between one who has only faith and one who translates his faith into works. We all know the final sentence of that dialogue, which is made up of a series of arguments and rebuttals: "A body dies when it is separated from the spirit; and in the same way faith, if it is separated from good deeds, is dead." Or, as an earlier verse says, "quite dead."[131]

53. Obviously, the works that John, Paul, and James refer to are

126 2 Thes. 1:11.
127 1 Tim. 1:5.
128 Phil. 5:6.
129 1 John 3:23.
130 1 John 4:7-8.
131 James, 2:17 and 26.

very different. They include piety, rectitude, patience, courage in giving witness, use of the gifts of the Spirit. But they also refer very explicitly to charity: "Anyone who says, "I love God," and hates his brother, is a liar, since a man who does not love the brother that he can see cannot love God, whom he has never seen.... Whoever believes that Jesus is the Christ has been begotten by God; and whoever loves the Father that begot him loves the child whom he begets."[132] Included too—many unfortunately forget this!—is the observance of God's commandments, as John himself reminds us in a complementary text: "We can be sure that we love God's children if we love God himself and do what he-has commanded us."[133] So unshakable is his conviction that he adds immediately: "This is the victory over the world—our faith." A faith that works through charity. For if faith without works is not real faith, the converse is also true: Charity without faith is not charity, either. For Paul this is incontestable. His entire argumentation against Israel is based precisely on the insufficiency of works founded on the law, now that the hour of faith has come. What gives them value is faith: "The pagans who were not looking for righteousness found it all the same, a righteousness that comes of faith, while Israel, looking for a righteousness derived from law, failed to do what that law required. Why did they fail? Because they relied on good deeds instead of trusting in faith."[134]

54. This Pauline criterion and analysis are still profoundly applicable today. I know very well that in the text Paul is referring to justification. But it still has all its value inasmuch as it condemns a salvation that we human beings strive to obtain—and to impose on others—on the basis of works, the assertion of rights and the imposition of obligations. We forget that it is faith that justifies, that makes us free, that blossoms into charity and gives meaning to our works. Faith without works is a dead faith. But works without faith, and without charity vitalizing it, are no more than well-meaning humanitarianism, philanthropy. To try to resolve the staggering problems of today with economic, technological, or political solutions

132 1 John 4:19 to 5:1.
133 1 John 5:2-4.
134 Rom. 9:30-32.

that lack a faith infused with charity, is to accumulate works upon works, but not 'sicut oportet,' [not in the manner required if they are to be supernaturally saving]. At best, such solutions settle or mitigate only superficial levels and material facets of the problem. But they leave the nucleus of the problem untouched; they do not reach the depths of man nor recognize his most profound values, the stifling or denial of which is the origin of the problem.

C. Charity and justice

55. The universal cry for justice is a 'sign of the times': Hundreds of millions of men and women of every continent and race, living in the most varied situations, are crying out for justice. If we listen to the other camp, the one that enacts the laws and defines what is just, it would seem that everything, or almost everything, has been done in the best possible way that circumstances permit. And yet, never has it been so clear as today that juridical edicts are inadequate to satisfy this hunger and thirst for justice. When law is divorced from morality, justice loses its ethical dimension and is fragmented into partial and subjective 'justices'. The conception of law held by quite a few modern states is not far from "ius, quia iussum," ["a law, because it has been enacted as a law"], thus sanctioning the divorce between what is legal and what is just. Of itself, statutory law alone cannot be the source of rights, for there are rights antecedent to all laws, and there is justice wherever even a single such right exists. When a God-given right is disregarded or repressed by a 'legal' injustice, it provokes the reaction of an illegal 'justice'. Not every legal justice is objectively just. To reduce the distance that separates justice from law is one of the prime objectives of any social and authentically human progress. But that can never be achieved as long as law and justice are not infused with charity.

56. There is an apparent charity, though, that is a mere cloak for injustice, when people are given, apart from the law and as if by benevolence, what is their due in justice. It is almsgiving as a subterfuge. We see many instances of these two aberrations today: spurious justice and spurious charity. Tyrannical regimes that impose laws violating rights, and paternalistic systems that offer

'charitable' aid programs instead of a clear policy of justice, are evils that make impossible the establishment of brotherhood and peace among men. Law, rights, and justice cannot be separated. Nor can they prescind from charity. The document issued by the Synod of 1971, entitled Justice in the World, says: "Love of neighbor and justice are inseparable. Love is above all a require-ment of justice, that is, an acknowledgment of the dignity and of the rights of one's neighbor." One cannot act justly without love. Even when we resist injustice we cannot prescind from love, since the universality of love is, by the express desire of Christ, a com-mandment that admits of no exceptions.

57. Well then, what is the precise relationship between charity and justice? John Paul II has explained this in his encyclical "Dives in Misericordia." "Love conditions justice, so to speak, and ultimately justice is the servant of charity."[135] Obviously, the pro-motion of justice is indispensable, because it is the first step to charity. To claim justice sometimes seems revolutionary, a subver-sive claim. And yet, it is so small a request: We really ought to ask for more, we should go beyond justice, to crown it with charity. Justice is necessary, but it is not enough. Charity adds its transcen-dent, inner dimension to justice and, when it has reached the limit of the realm of justice, can keep going even further. Because justice has its limits, and stops where rights terminate; but love has no boundaries because it reproduces, on our human scale, the in-finiteness of the divine essence and gives to each of our human brothers a claim to our unlimited service.

58. That is why anyone who has assimilated Christ's teaching and lives it radically cannot be satisfied with resisting injustice and promoting justice on an immanent human plane, but must of necessity be moved to do this out of love. The Church has made enormous progress in its understanding of the relationship between the exercise of justice and the practice of charity, and more and more it sees them as inseparable. Because justice is not measured only by one's obligation, but has to take cognizance of others' rights and needs; moreover, our concept of man, his values and his

135 Pope John Paul II, *Dives in Misericordia,* no. 4.

rights has progressed considerably. The Church's teachings on religious freedom and on the relations between Church, state, and society, are but one example of this evolution. The Church fixes its gaze ever more deeply on man, for in him it meets Christ. Man is indivisible. The rights that flow from his human nature, which are the object of justice, blend with his right to charity in virtue of his being image and son of God. Working for the re-establishment of justice where it is lacking is a Christian duty. If we failed to meet this challenge, our charity would be essentially and radically deficient—in hibernation, so to speak. The wounds that our brothers suffer by being deprived of basic rights would in such a case not make us feel their pain, nor evoke in us a 'brotherly' response. We would be accomplices in the 'sin of the world' and we would have failed to follow Paul's bidding: "Do not model yourselves on the behavior of the world around you, but let your behavior change, modelled by your new mind. This is the only way to discover the will of God and know what is good, what it is that God wants, what is the perfect thing to do."[136] That 'sin of the world' is injustice, and the 'great commandment of the world' is the love that Christ proclaimed.

59. There is a difference—though we are sometimes hard put to define it exactly—between justice and charity. The task of justice is to carry out clearly-defined works which can be the object of a contract, and the execution of which can be verified. These are obligations that do not require a man's dedication, but only his concrete acts. There is only one virtue that requires a man's whole being, that involves him in his entirety: love. Love is not the object of a contract, nor a task to be accomplished within a fixed time; it is not an added quality, but a vital force that is nourished by the very fact of being put into action. Love for one's neighbor gives not only this or that—as justice does—but one's whole self, and is expressed in concrete acts of the other virtues: beneficence (which gives to another of one's own), or justice (which gives him what is his own), or charity (by which one gives oneself).

60. Anyone who wants a listing—even if not exhaustive—of the

---

136 Rom. 12:2.

other part of the world...who in this life go about so cut off from one another for the sake of His love."[79] Xavier was so conscious of the distance that separated him from Ignatius that he used to sign his letters calling himself "the youngest son in the farthest exile."[80] This Xavier it is who felt himself intimately united with all the brethren by the bonds of love and affection. He writes to Ignatius: "When I read the last consoling words of your letter, that is, 'All yours, without ever being able to forget you, Ignatius,' as I read them with tears, so now with tears do I write, calling to mind...how much you have always loved me and still do love me...."[81] Not in Rome, but from a post far away on mission, was written that incomparable phrase: "It seems to me that Society of Jesus really means society of love and harmony of minds and hearts."[82] Its author, Xavier, had not read the *Constitutions,* which then had not yet been written. But he had lived with Ignatius.

29. To foster this mutual knowledge and love among the scattered brethren was one of Ignatius's constant preoccupations as the Society kept spreading out over the continents of Europe and Asia. Nadal knew that part of his own mission was to collaborate in this task, for in it was involved the whole sense of belonging and union itself. "Love makes us know the Society in a practical way," he said to the young scholastics of Alcalá. "To this and what helps is, love for the Institute itself, that you love the whole Society, those in the Indies, in Germany, in Italy and all those who belong to this Society, and that there be union and brotherhood among all as among the members of one and the same body. It is this love that makes all that exists in the Society pleasant and easy."[83]

6. Love that preserves the Society and makes it grow

30. The union of minds and hearts, born of love, is the condition for the preservation and growth of the Society, "not only of the

---

79 Cochin, Jan. 20, 1548, in *EppXav,* I, 395.
80 Cochin, Jan. 29, 1552, in *EppXav,* II, 293.
81 Ibid., II, 287.
82 Cochin, Jan. 12, 1549, in *EppXav,* II, 8.
83 Nadal, Exhortation 5 of 1561 at Alcalá, *Comme n tarii de Instituto.,* in *MonNad,* V, 348.

human rights in whose enforcement or promotion charity ought to assist justice, and even go beyond it, need do no more than page through the document 'The Promotion of Human Rights: An Evangelical Requirement in the Ministry', issued by the Synod of 1974. Dignity and human rights find their fullest expression in the gospel, say the Synod Bishops. And we may add that our knowledge of the extent of human rights is far from being complete. Just as we still do not know the limit of man's physical capacities, as seemingly unbeatable records keep falling, so we cannot determine what a thoroughly developed moral conscience and a sense of Christian brotherhood and equality will some day affirm to be the full scope of human rights. The history of labor and social movements shows this only too clearly. Respect for man's rights and duties is, Vatican II tells us, what constitutes the common good.[137] The 1948 Universal Declaration of Human Rights gives a long list of basic rights, and subsequent international pacts apply those rights to particular areas. The scope of justice is clear, then. But does not our increasingly clear knowledge of what are the rights to which justice is correlative, when contrasted with the extremely bitter reality we see around us, reveal a disillusioning contradiction between our hopes and that reality? Only charity can, by seeing to it that justice is applied in all its amplitude, keep injustice from erupting in the tragic violence that we must constantly deplore.

D. Charity a higher form of justice

61. Justice then, even justice based on law and on rights, is not everywhere and always enough. There are versions of justice that take no account of the concrete existential situation of the persons and conditions to which it is applied. There are kinds of justice that are a cover-up for vested interests. A justice, a law that demands too little, leaves the helpless or oppressed man defenseless. So too, a violent law, a violent justice that demands too much, can become a hangman's noose for everyone. And even a justice with all the guarantees of equity can, if mercilessly applied, be inhuman. "The

---

137 Vatican II, on Religious Liberty, no. 6; The Church in the Modern World, nos. 26 and 73.

experience of the past and of our own time demonstrates that justice alone is not enough, that is can even lead to the negation and destruction of itself, if that deeper power, which is love, is not allowed to shape human life in its various dimensions. It has been precisely historical experience that, among other things, has led to the formulation of the saying: *summum ius, summa iniuria.*"[138] This sort of justice is not what Christ came to bring to the world. By the law, we were all condemned. But the justice of Christ went beyond the law, motivated as it was by charity. This is the charity that among men must complement justice, making it a higher sort of justice. It is the only one that can go on, beyond mere justice, to the point of meeting the needs of men. For its scope, going beyond the slogans of "equality for all" and "to each according to his merits," reaches out "to each according to his needs," which is the only truly human and Christian norm. That higher form of justice, which is charity, will have a preferential care for the poor, the weak, and the oppressed in the name of a strict right that, without charity, could turn out to be a *summa iniuria.*[139]

62. The equity of justice has nothing to fear from charity, on condition that justice protect and defend all of man's rights, because its equity not only does not lessen its impartiality, but makes it even more perceptive and clear-sighted, enabling it to appreciate the human and vital depths of every situation and to act accordingly. That is what we mean by asserting that charity is a higher form of justice, with a far loftier perspective, one that soars up to the heights of the divine justice itself, which is all charity and mercy. And with a more penetrating scope too, since it plunges down to the inmost depths of man, to his pain, his need, his helplessness, which are realities that are lost sight of when he is treated impersonally, as a mere subject of the law.

63. This is that higher form of justice which Christ promulgated in his Good News. John Paul II has given clear prominence to this concept in his "Dives in Misericordia," when commenting on the parable of the Prodigal Son in Luke's Gospel. We all know what the

---

138 *Dives in Misericordia,* no. 12.
139 Edouard Hamel, "La miséricorde, une sorte de justice supérieure?" in *Studia Moralia* (1977), 585.

Gospel of John tells us in this regard. And it is significant that another evangelist, Matthew, in the three passages where he uses the word 'eleos', compassionate charity, always contrasts it with legal prescriptions. "Alas for you, scribes and pharisees, you hypocrites! You who pay your tithe of mint and dill and cummin and have neglected the weightier matters of the law—justice, mercy, good faith!"[140] Against the reproach of breaking the law by eating with publicans and sinners, Jesus defends himself by citing a text of Hosea: "Go and learn the meaning of the words: What I want is mercy, not sacrifice."[141] When the pharisees accuse his disciples of violating the law of the sabbath, Jesus replies that this law can conflict with another, even higher law: that of mercy.[142] So clear is this that in extreme cases, necessity has gained entrance into the law by the door of *epikeia*. The duty of helping someone who has suffered disaster, say by offering our services, can in fact oblige us even though it may involve a violation of lesser laws. Charity at times becomes a matter of strict justice.

E. The social dimension of charity

64. Charity has a social dimension, deriving not only from the universality of charity but also from man's social condition. Charity on a merely personal basis is not enough. In a world like today's, which is growing more and more socialized, where man finds himself caught in the mesh of socio-economic and political structures of every sort, charity has to be understood and put into practice on a social scale as well. On this social level charity is of less immediate effects and perhaps less rewarding; it is more anonymous and more long-range before its results become apparent. But, except in emergency cases, it is more effective. It aims precisely at improving those structures on which depends the welfare of groups of our fellow men who have particular needs and wants. This is a charity that must almost of necessity look for help from institutions and organizations that, by their action on structures, can modify the complex factors that affect the common good. No juridical

---

140 Matt. 23:23.
141 Matt. 9:12.
142 Matt. 12:7.

order is beyond improvement. In all of them there is room for betterment, so that social charity, working through social justice and going beyond it, becomes operative. The danger in even the best designed human structures is their rigidity. The stability that we strive to give them is both their strength and their weakness, for their inflexibility and immutability can make them oppressive. Charity, with its dynamism that impels it to go beyond the law and with its independence of all political ties, is the best corrective against the rigid hardening to which all systems and structures are doomed. Charity is the vanguard of justice.

65. Let us not exaggerate, however. Not every structure is necessarily unjust. Indeed, structures are necessary, and each new conquest in charity has to be integrated into a structure, modifying it and making it flexible and progressive. Such charity, social in its purpose, must be social in its agents too. That is, it must arise from a social group, which for us means from the people of God, embracing all of us. It is a duty arising from our common faith, from our sharing in divine sonship and from the fact that we are brothers. We are bound by our solidarity and coresponsibility. The Lord, who praises the individual charity of the Good Samaritan, has made it quite clear that he refuses to let personal charity be an excuse for omitting charity towards the group, and that he does not accept a merely individualistic statement of the problem, as in "When did we see you [in the singular] hungry or thirsty" and the rest? Christ focuses on the need of the group as such when he uses the category: the 'little ones'. And he gives his reason in these two words "my brothers."[143] Precisely because man integrates his individual personality in the social reality of the Kingdom, and because all men are called to it,[144] the law of charity, which Christ typified as the law of his Kingdom, has to bear in mind our social condition; there has to be a social charity. This social charity is the peak expression of 'agape', that disinterested, anonymous, long-range love, for its own sake as well as for the love of God, that has been placed in our hearts.

66. When the 32nd General Congregation, with its supreme

143 Matt. 25:31-46.
144 Rom. 11:25.

authority, defined in a decree how the phrase "for the defense and propagation of the faith" in our Formula of the Institute is to be· translated to apply to the concrete situation of today's world, it was aware that countless men and women everywhere on earth are being denied justice. It therefore interpreted the "defense and propagation of the faith"—or "being a Jesuit today," which is the same thing—as meaning "to engage under the standard of the cross, in the crucial struggle of our time: the struggle for faith and that struggle for justice which it includes."[145] The process by which the Society arrived at that formulation was much like the conversion process of the *Exercises* and followed the same dynamic of total, loving, and distinguished surrender to Christ's cause. The Society acknowledged its past deficiencies in the service of faith and the promotion of justice, and asked itself, before Christ crucified, what it has done for him and what it should do for him, and at the feet of Christ crucified out of love it chose participation in this struggle for faith and justice as the focal point that identifies what Jesuits today are and do.

67. That decision seemed a great step forward, and the Society has been striving since then to carry it out. We still need perspective to evaluate the current balance of well-meant failures and undeniable successes which that option has produced in the Church through the Society. In the light of the most recent encyclical, "Dives in Misericordia," we may say that, with all the imperfections of any human choice, it was an option in the right direction. However, this is not sufficient, it is not the last step. The Congregation realized that charity is the 'final step' and basis of everything, and that true justice starts from and is crowned in charity. "There is no genuine conversion to the love of God without conversion to the love of neighbor and, therefore, to the demands of justice. Hence, fidelity to our apostolic mission requires that we propose the whole of Christian salvation and lead others to embrace it. Christian salvation consists in an undivided love of the Father and of the neighbor and of justice. Since evangelization is proclamation of that faith which is made operative in love of others, the promo-

---

145 General Congregation 32, decree 2, no. 2 (hereafter abbreviated GC 32, 2:2).

tion of justice is indispensable to it."[146] Further on in that same Decree 4, the Congregation affirmed: "If the promotion of justice is to attain its ultimate end, it should be carried out in such a way as to bring men and women to desire and to welcome the eschatological freedom and salvation offered to us by God in Christ. The methods we employ and the activities we undertake should express the spirit of the Beatitudes and bring people to a real reconciliation."[147] We should keep these paragraphs of Decree 4 well in mind, so that our reading of it will not be incomplete, slanted, and unbalanced. The Society still has to advance in its understanding of, and search for, that justice which it has pledged itself to promote. I am sure the effort will lead us to discover an even wider field—that of charity.

F. 'Agape' versus 'anomia'

68. Yes, justice is not enough. The world needs a stronger cure, a more effective witness and more effective deeds: those of love. When we glance over the newspaper headlines and seek somehow for the real reason why human relations are at such a low ebb—within the family, the state, the world of work, the economic order, and internationally—every explanation in terms of justice and injustice seems inadequate. Never have people talked so much about justice, and yet never has justice been so flagrantly disregarded. This reminds me of the scene with which Matthew begins the apocalyptic section of his Gospel.[148] It is a short literary sketch, drawn with strong and expressive strokes. It contains one verse that is worth its weight in gold, a deep, stark, and accurate explanation of what is happening today: "such will be the spread of wickedness, that love in most men will grow cold."[149] Wickedness and love are expressed in the original Greek by the two words: 'anomia' and 'agape'. The two grow in inverse proportion one to the other. It is important to dwell a while on these two concepts.

69. 'Anomia' is, as many versions translate it, wickedness.

146 GC 32, 4:28.
147 GC 32, 4:33.
148 Matt. 24:4-14.
149 Matt. 24:12.

Literally, it is the total absence of law, or the violation and scorn of law. It is the exaltation of selfishness with no regard at all for the norm, the flouting of law; in a word, injustice. It is the repetition of that primeval pride which led to man's fall—the first sin—and which keeps sin in the world even today. In the gospel text just quoted, 'anomia' is related to the chaos described in the preceding lines: wars, famines, calamities, false rumors. Men, who are at once promoters and victims of this anomia, compound the evils: false redeemers, treachery, desertion, widespread hatred. These are the disastrous consequences of the disregard for justice, of the protection of one's own interests to the detriment of others' rights and needs, and the detriment of the common good. The right of might replaces the might of right: it nullifies God's command, revealed in Jesus, that love and brotherhood should rule the relationships among men. It is, in the technical sense, the rule of immorality, ethical degeneration. Anomia is the absence of justice, iniquity in its etymological sense: the absence of equity, injustice.

70. 'Agape' (a favourite word with John, but one that in Matthew appears only in this text) is disinterested love, the urge to self-giving that our benevolence towards others prompts us to. It is the word that aptly expresses God's love for us. It is the sort of love among human beings that Christ termed his commandment, the new commandment. It is the sign that we have 'known' the Father. For those who do not believe, it is the guarantee and test of the faith that is alive in us. Agape-love, in contradistinction to 'eros', is the center around which history is unified, just as anomia is its divisive factor. Because, we must remember, although 'agape' is the term for both man's love of God and his love for his brothers, we are using it here in the second sense. This is clear by the fact that it is contrasted with anomia, and evident from the content of this entire eschatological section of Matthew, which ends precisely by exalting love and charity towards our brothers as the criterion of sifting at the Last Judgment.[150]

71. Agape and anomia are antithetical. Matthew centers the cosmic distress of the final age on this duel between anomia-

---

150 Matt. 25:31-46.

wickedness-injustice and agape-love. Anomia: we seem to be reading the chronicle of contemporary history. An assault on man, an arbitrary and violent imposition of authority over persons, indifference towards people's needs, a merciless and blind justice: injustice. Agape: a disinterested impulse that leads us to understand, to empathize, to share, to help and to heal, born of faith in the love that God has for us and that we see revealed in our brothers. That love is still being given in today's world. As Nadal used to say, it is a flame that has always been lit, and still is, in the Church and in our least Society, and that we strive to keep alive and quicken. A flame that is a beacon, a sign of hope, a light for our way, and warmth for our hearts. Love unites, anomia divides. Matthew shows these two forces in a permanent state of combat, in an apocalyptic crescendo. Anomia is the substantial, historical, and cosmic injustice that undermines the gospel-inspired basis of human relations. Agape is the evangelical message of love and of peace, all that gives meaning to the life that is born of faith, both personal and communitarian or social.

72. The message of Matthew leaves the door open to hope: *He who perseveres to the end will be saved.* Persevering despite adverse forces, despite others' incomprehension, despite our own discouragement. In order to overcome, we must persevere in the love of charity that is linked to our faith and calls for the promotion of justice. This charity is the world's only real hope for salvation. To persevere, that is the watchword in Mark's Gospel too[151] and in Luke's: "You will be saved if you persevere."[152]

73. I am firmly convinced that the Society, in virtue of the Trinitarian inspiration of its Ignatian charism, rooted and grounded in love, is providentially prepared to enter the struggle and be engaged effectively in curbing the spread of anomia and working for the victory of love. The plight of the world, I can confidently assert, so deeply wounds our sensibilities as Jesuits that it sets the inmost fibers of our apostolic zeal a-tingling. Our historical mission is involved in all this, for the purpose of our Society is the

151 Mark 13:13.
152 Luke 21:19.

defense and propagation of the faith, and we know that faith moves and is moved by charity, and that charity brings about and goes beyond justice. The struggle for faith, the promotion of justice, the commitment to charity, all these are our objective, and in it lies our raison d'être. Our updated renewal ("accommodata renovatio") consists in letting ourselves be imbued by this idea and in living it with all the intensity of the Ignatian 'magis'. In this way we shall have reached the ultimate source of Ignatius's Trinitarian charism: the divine essence, which is love.

★ ★ ★

74. Let me end now greeting you all, as well as every Jesuit who will read these pages, with that wonderful Pauline formula: "Peace be to the brethren, and love with faith, from God the Father and the Lord Jesus Christ. Grace be with all who love our Lord Jesus Christ with love undying."[153]

III. THE HEART OF JESUS, RESUME AND SYMBOL OF LOVE

Having reached this point, when we see that love is the very core of Christian—and therefore Ignatian—spirituality, I feel somewhat obliged to add a final consideration.

A. *Love as a synthesis*

75. What I have said so far may be synthesized as follows:

1. Love (service) for our brothers, for Christ, for the Father, is the single and indivisible object of our charity.

2. Love resolves the dichotomies and tensions that can arise in an imperfectly understood Ignatian spirituality. For instance:

—— *The tension between faith and justice* is resolved in charity. Faith has to be informed by charity, "fides informata caritate," and so too must justice, which thus becomes a higher form of justice: It is charity that calls for justice.

—— *The tension between one's own and one's neighbor's perfection.* Both should be the perfection of one and the same

---

153 Eph. 6:23-24.

charity, which tends to keep growing, as well intensively in itself, as extensively in the spread to and perfection of our fellow men.

—— *The tension between prayer and active apostolic work* is resolved in the "contemplativus in actione," in seeking God in all things (the Contemplation for Attaining Love).

—— *The tension among the three religious vows* disappears when their motivation and observance are inspired and impelled by charity (the same can be said of the fourth vow).

—— *The tension between discernment and obedience.* Charity should be present both at the origin and in the final goal of discernment: The presence of this 'agape' enables us to discern God's will (Rom 12:2), it is an intuition of charity (Eph 3:18-19; Col 2:2). Obedience similarly is an expression of that same divine will. Both superior and subject ought to be animated by charity, with the intuitiveness that is proper to love (Therrien: *Le discernement dans les écrits pauliniens,* p. 179).

3. Love is the solution to the apostolic problems created by the wickedness (anomia) of today's world.

4. Love is the very depth of the personality and work of Jesus Christ, that which gives unity to it all.

5. Love is also the deepest element of our life and activity, since with Jesus Christ we share one common Spirit (the Person, who is love), who makes us cry out like Christ: Abba, Father!

Love, then, understood in all its depth and breadth (both charity and mercy), is the synthesis of the whole life of Jesus Christ, and should be that of the Jesuit's whole life too.

76. Now, the natural symbol of love is the heart. The heart of Christ, therefore, is the natural symbol for representing and inspiring our personal and institutional spirituality, leading us to the very source and abyss of the human-divine love of Jesus Christ.

B. Devotion to the Heart of Christ—symbolizes and expresses the core of the Ignatian charism

77. And so, at the close of this address, I would like to tell the Society something that I believe I should not pass over in silence.

From my noviceship on, I have always been convinced that in the so-called "Devotion to the Sacred Heart" there is summed up a symbolic expression of the very core of the Ignatian spirit and an extraordinary power—"ultra quam speraverint"—both for personal perfection and for apostolic fruitfulness. This conviction is still mine today. It may have surprised some that during my generalate I have said relatively little on this topic. There was a reason for it, which we might call pastoral. In recent decades the very phrase "the Sacred Heart" has not failed to provoke emotional and allergic reactions in some, partly perhaps as a reaction to forms of presentation and terminology linked with tastes of a bygone age. So I thought it advisable to let some time go by, in the certainty that that attitude, more emotional than rational, would gradually change.

I cherished, and still do cherish, the conviction that the immense value of so deep a spirituality—which the popes have termed excellent,[154] which employs so universal and so human a biblical symbol,[155] and a word, "heart," that is a genuine source-word or key word (*Urwort*)—would before long come back into usage.

C. My writings on this topic, and my silence

78. For this reason, much to my regret, I have spoken and written relatively little on this subject, although I have often mentioned it in private conversation with individuals and find in this devotion one of the most profound affective sources of my interior life.

79. As I bring to an end this series of conferences on the Ignatian charism, I could not but give the Society an explanation for this silence of mine, which I trust will be understood. And at the same time, I did not wish to draw the pall of silence over my deep conviction that all of us, as the Society of Jesus, should reflect and discern before Christ crucified what this devotion has meant for the Society, and what it should mean even today. In today's circumstances, the world offers us challenges and opportunities that can be fully met only with the power of this love of the Heart of Christ.

---

154 See Leo XIII, *Annum Sacrum*, 1899; Pius XI, *Miserentissimus Redemptor*, 1928; Pius XII, *Haurietis Aquas*, 1956; Paul VI, *Investigabiles Divitias Christi*, 1965.

155 Eph. 1:18.

D. My final message on the Heart of Jesus

80. This is the message that I wanted to communicate to you. There is no question of seeking to force or impose anything in an area where love precisely is involved. But I do wish to say: Give thought to this message, and "ponder on what presents itself to your mind."[156] It would be sad if, having so great a treasure in our spirituality, even our institutional spirituality, we were to leave it aside for largely specious reasons.

81. If you want my advice, I would say to you, after fifty-three years of living in the Society and almost sixteen of being its General, that there is a tremendous power latent in this devotion to the Heart of Christ. Each of us should discover it for himself—if he has not already done so—and then, entering deeply into it, apply it to his personal life in whatever way the Lord may suggest and grant. There is here an extraordinary grace that God offers us.

82. The Society needs the power (*dynamis*) contained in this symbol and in the reality that it proclaims: the love of the Heart of Christ. Perhaps what we need is an act of ecclesial humility, to accept what the Supreme Pontiffs, the General Congregations, and the Generals of the Society have incessantly repeated. And yet, I am convinced that there could be few proofs of the spiritual renewal of the Society so clear as a widespread and vigorous devotion to the Heart of Jesus. Our apostolate would receive new strength and we would see its effects very soon, both in our personal lives and in our apostolic activities.

83. Let us not fall into the presumptuous temptation of considering ourselves superior to a devotion that is expressed in a symbol or in a graphic representation of it. Let us not join "the wise and prudent of this world" from whom the Father keeps hidden his truths and mysteries, while he reveals them to those who are or make themselves *little ones.* "[157] Let us have that simplicity of heart which is the first condition for a profound conversion: "Unless you

156 *SpEx*, [53].
157 Luke 11:21; Matt. 11:25.

change and make yourselves like little children..."[158] Those are Christ's words, and we might translate them in this way: "If you want, as individuals and as a Society, to enter into the treasures of the Kingdom and to help build it up with an extraordinary effectiveness, make yourselves like the poor whom you wish to serve. You keep on saying so often that the poor have taught you more than many books; learn from them, then, this very simple lesson: Acknowledge my love in my Heart."

158 Matt. 18:3.